WORTHY AS FUCK
From One Crazy Bitch To Another
By Brandee Kocsis

© 2025 Brandee Kocsis
ISBN: 978-1-0696125-0-2
All rights reserved.
No part of this publication may be reproduced, stored in a retrieval system, or transmitted in any form or by any means, electronic, mechanical, photocopying, recording, or otherwise, without the prior written permission of the author.

Disclaimer

This book is a memoir based on true events as experienced by the author. Names and identifying details have been changed or omitted to protect the privacy of individuals. Any resemblance to real persons, living or dead, is purely coincidental. The events are described from the author's personal perspective and are not intended to malign or defame any individual or group.

The author does not assume responsibility for how the content is interpreted or used by others. The insights, opinions, and experiences shared in this book are meant for educational and personal growth purposes only.

This is my story. These are my truths.

CHAPTER 1 Hoover This Bitch

CHAPTER 2

The Relationship That Broke Me (So I Could Rebuild Me)

Chapter 3

Shattered Crowns & Fake Kings

Chapter 4: The Silent Shame of a 'Broken' Body

Chapter 5: Nice Guys, Red Flags, and Red Wine

CHAPTER 6: The Perception; You belong To Me

CHAPTER 7: Gaslight, Girlboss, Grieve, Repeat

Chapter 8: It's Not Mothering, It's a Fucking Boundary!

Chapter 9: Addicted To The Apology that Never Came

Chapter 10: The Aftermath: I Am Not Enough

Chapter 11: What The Fuck Wellness

Chapter 12: Motherhood And Guilt: The Unpaid Internship From Hell

Chapter 13: This Is What Love Looks Like (After The Wreckage)

Chapter 14: Burn The Rulebook, Rewire The Truth.

Chapter 15: The Childhood Wounds They Said Weren't That Bad

Chapter 16: Healing The Mirror: Rebuilding The Self Trust

Chapter 17: The Betrayal Was Never About You (But Healing Always Is)

Chapter 18: Burned By Love, Reborn In Truth

Chapter 19: Reclaiming Your Body, Food, And Fucking Sanity

CHAPTER 20: Boundary Breakdowns & the Bullshit We Swallow

Chapter 21: Comparison Is A Thieving Little Bitch

CHAPTER 22: Silent as a MOTHERfucker – The Guilt No One Talks About

FINAL GOODBYE: One Last Fuck You To Who You Use To Be

THE FINAL AFFIRMATION

Dear Reader,

Acknowledgments

About the Author

Dedication

To my daughter—
You are the reason I do this.
I never want you to question your worth, shrink yourself for anyone, or dim your damn light to make others feel more comfortable.
You are bold. You are fierce. You are powerful as fuck.
And even when life knocks you on your ass—and it will—I want you to know this:
You will never lose your worth. Not ever.
I made a shit-ton of mistakes so I could show you that we don't break—we rebuild. And we come back louder, stronger, and even more unapologetic.

To my mom—
Thank you for always supporting my chaos, cheering on my shenanigans, and saying "okay!" to every random-ass idea I ever had (even when you probably wanted to run).
You've been my sounding board, my soft place to land, and my hype girl before that was even a thing.
Love you forever.

To my ride-or-die tribe—
My girlfriends. My soul sisters. My circle of badassery.
You've seen me through every meltdown, glow-up, rock bottom, and "WTF am I doing with my life" moment.
From ugly crying to drive-by vent sessions to wild-ass dreams you never questioned—
Thank you for never making me feel too much.
You showed up. You held space. You passed the tequila. I love you.

To my dad—
You're not here anymore, but your voice is still in my head.
You always told me I could do whatever the hell I wanted—and if I was gonna be stupid, I had to be tough.
Spoiler alert: I was. And I am.

I love you, Dad. This one's for you.
And to YOU—
Yeah, you holding this book like it's about to slap your soul (it is):
This is for every woman who's ever felt like she wasn't enough.
This is for the ones who are done settling, done playing small, and done watering themselves down.
This is for the women who are ready to get loud, take up space, and own every damn part of who they are.
To being bold.
To being messy.
To being Worthy as Fuck

Let's fucking go.

With all the love,
Brandee

PREFACE
Read this before the world catches up to who the fuck you are.*

If you're holding this book, one of two things has probably happened:

You hit a rock bottom so loud it echoed in your bones.
You looked in the mirror and said, "I can't keep living like this."

Either way, welcome. You just made the best damn decision of your life.

Let me introduce myself properly.

I'm Brandee —nurse by trade, disruptor by design, and full-blown Mindset Alchemist by divine assignment. What's that mean? It means I help people—especially women—burn down the bullshit stories they were handed and rebuild an identity rooted in radical self-worth, truth, and unapologetic AF power.
I'm not a life coach.
I'm not a motivational speaker.
And I sure as hell am not your typical self-help author.
I'm the woman who tells you the truth when you're still trying to sugarcoat the wound.
I don't do fluff.
I don't do "love and light."
I do rage, resurrection, and real fucking healing.
I wrote this book because I lived this book.
Every chapter you're about to read.
I bled through it. I sobbed through it. I questioned my sanity, my worth, my mothering, my marriage, my femininity—hell, my entire identity—to get here.

I've buried versions of myself I used to beg people to love.
I've walked through heartbreaks that nearly took me out.

I've been the woman who stayed too long, shrank too small, and silenced her soul just to feel "safe."

But I made it out.
And now I'm on a mission to make sure you do too.

This isn't a memoir.
It's a revolution in book form.

A war cry for every woman who was told she had to be quiet, soft, desirable, likeable, "not too much," and "never a bürden."

A love letter to every mother who's ever cried in the bathroom while dinner burned, wondering if she was fucking her kid up just by existing in survival mode.

A slap-in-the-face and a hand on your back for the woman who secretly knows she was meant for more but doesn't know where to start.

Here's what I want you to know:

Healing doesn't look like bubble baths and moon water.
It looks like crying in your car outside therapy.
It looks like rewriting the story you were told about your worth.
It looks like saying, "Not this time, motherfucker," to your trauma.

That's what this book is.

It's your mirror, your permission slip, your fuck-it button, and your sacred fucking scripture for becoming Worthy AF.

I am not perfect. I am not always polished. But I am real.
And in a world of highlight reels and copy-paste coaches, real wins.

So if you're ready to laugh, cry, throw the book across the room, and then pick it back up and whisper, "Holy shit, she's talking about me…"—
Then let's fucking go.

This isn't a book you read once.
This is a book you become.

—Brandee
Certified Worthy AF
Mindset Alchemist | Nurse | Cycle-Breaker | Truth-Teller | Vibe so loud you can't ignore it

LET'S FUCKING BEGIN

This isn't a self-help book.
This is a fucking wake-up call.

If you picked this up thinking I was going to gently hold your hand and whisper affirmations while you manifest your dream life without doing the work—buckle up, sweetheart.

You're not here to be babied.
You're here to burn the goddamn rulebook.

You've spent long enough trying to be the "good girl," the perfect wife, the always-available friend, the woman who smiles even when she's dying inside.

Enough.
You weren't born to be palatable.

You were born to be powerful.

This book is your permission slip to say:

Fuck the shame.
Fuck the silence.
Fuck the systems that told you your worth was up for debate.
Here's what's waiting for you in these pages:
Real stories.
 Ugly truths.
 Unfiltered breakthroughs.
 Swear words. (A lot of them.)

And the blueprint to rebuild your identity on truth, power, and radical self-worth.

So grab a pen, grab a highlighter, grab a drink—hell, grab your journal and a vibrator if that's what it takes—and settle in.

Because once you start reading, something inside you is going to crack open.
And you're not going to be able to un see your own fucking power ever again.

This isn't just a book.
It's a rebellion.
And it starts now.

Let's fucking begin.

CHAPTER 1 Hoover This Bitch

"The rumour wasn't true-but the shame sure as hell was"

"Hoover This, Bitch": How One Lie Fucked My Whole Identity (Until I Took That Shit Back)

Let me take you back.
Not to the beginning of the Pinterest-perfect story.
Not to the part where everything looks shiny and healed and filtered through an empowering quote.
I'm talking about the real beginning.
The one you tried to forget.
The one that cracked your self-worth like a goddamn egg on a hot sidewalk. For me? That story starts in high school. The place where insecurity gets passed around like Juicy Tubes lip gloss in a girls 'bathroom.
Where being liked mattered more than being honest. Where your identity could be ruined before lunch period by a single fucking rumor. And that's exactly what happened to me. Let me introduce you to the first version of me who ever felt broken. The girl who got called "crazy" before she ever raised her voice. The girl who's worth got yanked out from under her like a rug at a house party. Her name was Brandee. And she got a nickname that nearly destroyed her.

High School Hallways and Hit Jobs

I didn't walk into high school with big dreams of being the Regina George of my town.
I was just the new girl.
Moved to a tight-knit, small-town community in 1995— where best friends weren't made, they were inherited from kindergarten. If you didn't grow up on the same street as someone, you were a fucking outsider.
At first, I thought I'd found my crew. A few girls in the neighborhood introduced themselves. They invited me to a party. I was pumped. I had strict parents, so even getting the green light to go felt like a badge of honor.

I curled my bangs (this was the '90s, don't judge), slipped on the hottest Delia's-inspired outfit I could find, and strutted into that party thinking—okay, maybe I belong here.
I chatted. I flirted. I was friendly.
And then, one guy—you know the type: cocky, hot, and emotionally underdeveloped—decided that my friendliness was code for "I want to suck your dick."
Spoiler alert: I didn't.
I didn't go off with him.
I didn't kiss him.
I didn't touch him.
I didn't even like him like that.
But apparently, his ego couldn't handle the rejection. So he did what small men do: He made shit up.
Welcome to the Hoover Era
Monday morning, I walked into school with zero clue that my entire social life had been torched over the weekend.Whispers.Stares Smirks. Full-body cringe.And then I heard it.
"Yo, Hoover's here!"
I blinked. "What?"
"HOOVER," someone repeated, laughing. "Like the vacuum. Heard you sucked him off."
Oh.
Cool.
So that's how this week was going.

I stood frozen in the hallway, my heart pounding in my chest like it was trying to escape.
I didn't even know how to process it.It wasn't true.I knew it wasn't true.But that didn't matter.In high school, truth has no fucking currency. Only drama does. And if you've ever

been a teenage girl whose reputation got slaughtered by a lie…You know that something in you dies that day.For me? That day was the funeral for my trust in other people.
The girl who smiled at strangers? Dead.
The girl who made friends easily? Buried.
The girl who wanted to fit in? Cremated.
All that was left.
A new girl.
The cold one.
The quiet one.
The don't-fuck-with-me-or-I'll-burn-this-school-down-with-my-eyes one.
Resting bitch face? Born.
Hyper-vigilance? Installed.
Bitch armour? Activated.

You Don't Just Wake Up "Crazy"

Let's talk about that word.
Crazy.
That's the label girls get slapped with when they start acting like their pain matters. It's what people call you when you start enforcing boundaries or stop playing nice.
But let's be real:
You don't wake up crazy. You become crazy—after enough lies get told about you. After you see how fast people will believe something that didn't even fucking happen. After you realize no one is coming to defend you. No one asks your side of the story. Because the lie is more fun.
So, what do you do?
You adapt.
You become ice.
You sharpen your tongue.
You walk like your thighs could cut a bitch.
You armour the hell up.

Because in the world of small-town high school? Nice girls get eaten alive. And it wasn't just the guys who ran with the rumour. It was the girls.
That's the worst part.
It was the girls whispering behind locker doors, laughing during gym class, making jokes in group projects. Like my body, my name, my identity were just punchlines in their little "we're not like her" club.
They turned me into the villain of a story I never even auditioned for. So, like any teenage girl trying to survive, I did the only thing that felt safe…
I became the villain.

Fast-Forward: When the Wound Reopens

Years later—I'm a grown woman. A nurse. A mom. A whole-ass adult with a mortgage and matching Tupperware lids.
I walk into a party. And guess who's there? One of them. Same sneaky little smile. Same judgmental eyes. Like time hadn't moved at all. She whispers to someone across the table. I hear my name. My last name—like she was double-checking it was me. Like she was confirming a tabloid headline from 1997. And just like that—I was 16 again. Standing in that hallway. Face hot. Stomach flipping. Rage boiling.
Except now? I knew what to do. I didn't throw hands. I didn't cry. But I left. Not because I was weak.
Because I was done.
Done carrying shame that never fucking belonged to me.

Real Talk: People Project Their Shit

That woman didn't come for me because I mattered to her. She came for me because she doesn't matter to herself. She needed attention. Validation. A sense of superiority.
But what she actually did was spark a fire in me. Because what I know now? When people can't find a way to rise—

they try to pull down the ones who already have. And I am not their emotional support punching bag. Not anymore.

What the Rumour Didn't Know

The "Hoover" girl?

She grew up. She became a mother. A nurse. A fucking identity alchemist. She turned her trauma into power and wrote a damn book. She started a movement. A self-worth revolution.

And now?

She's helping women around the world suck the lies out of their stories like the fucking vacuums people once mocked her for. (See what I did there…)

Call it full circle. Call it revenge. I call it healing.

So, Let's Get Something Straight

You are not who they say you are.
You are not your worst rumour.
You are not your reputation.
You are not your trauma.
You are not the names you were called.
Not "bitch."
Not "crazy."
Not "too much."
You are the one who survived. You are the one who woke up today and chose to rise, again.
You are the author of your own fucking story now.
So, turn the page.
And say it with me, babe—
I am worthy as fuck.

Burn the Bullshit, Build the Truth

That party was the wake-up call I didn't know I still needed.

Because healing isn't always this perfect, sparkly Instagram moment where you do yoga at sunrise and whisper affirmations while sipping on moon water. Sometimes healing is messy AF. Sometimes it's realizing your triggers

still exist and your nervous system is on high alert the second your trauma gets called out by name.
But here's the thing:
I didn't walk out of that party because I was weak. I walked out because I was done letting ghosts fuck with my present.
The girl who walked out of that house wasn't Hoover. She was a grown-ass woman who had outlived the lie—and was finally ready to bury it.
Hoover Didn't Win. She Rewired.
Do you know what that moment gave me?
Clarity.
Clarity that I had never deserved the way I was treated.
Clarity that the nickname was never about me—it was about him trying to flex his fragile masculinity and keep his ego intact.
And let's be honest, the real fucking flex is growing into a woman who could walk into any room and not flinch when someone brings up your past.
That's power.
That's healing.
That's Worthy AF.
So, I started doing the work. Not the surface-level stuff. The real, soul-deep work. I sat with my triggers. I revisited the dressing room moments (yes, that stuck-in-the-shirt meltdown counts).
I wrote. I cried. I screamed. I journaled my rage, shame, grief, and every "fuck you" I never got to say out loud in high school. And I created something from it.
You're holding it now.
This book? This whole fucking movement? It was born from that pain. From that rumour. From that girl.
So yeah, Hoover didn't win.
She just ended up giving me my origin story.
Why We Laugh It Off (But Still Bleed Inside)

We make jokes about our trauma. We call ourselves "crazy." We toss out sarcastic one-liners like it's no big deal. But humour is often pain in disguise. It's how we survive. It's how we cope. It's how we soften the blow so we can keep showing up for work, for our kids, for our friends—even when we're unraveling on the inside.

The problem is, when we laugh too much, we start to believe the punchline.

"Maybe I am too much."
"Maybe I was asking for it."
"Maybe I should just get over it."
NO.

Let me be your loudest, sassiest, tequila-sipping best friend right now and say this with my whole damn chest: You don't owe anyone your silence just because they're uncomfortable with your truth. What happened to you was real. What it did to you was real. And the way it still shows up in your life? Also, real.

From Punchline to Powerhouse

So how do you go from being the punchline to reclaiming your fucking crown?

You name the lie.
You rewrite the story.
You own the narrative.

For years, my identity was handed to me by other people. Hoover. Cold. Bitchy. Too much.

Now?

I'm a damn powerhouse. I'm a nurse. A single mom. A fucking phoenix with mascara on. I'm the woman who walks into a room and doesn't shrink to make other people comfortable anymore.

I don't apologize for being too much—I warn people ahead of time. And if you're reading this, I know you've got your own "Hoover moment."

Your own story that tried to bury you in shame and keep you small.

But sis… that story? It's not you're ending. It's your fucking beginning.

Let's Get Real—Here's What You Need to Hear.

You don't become "crazy" out of nowhere. You become it because life tried to crush you, and your nervous system learned how to scream back. You don't become "too sensitive" because you cry. You become that way because no one ever let you cry safely. You don't become "difficult" because you set boundaries. You become that way because you were tired of being everyone's emotional doormat.

So, here's your permission slip:

To be loud.

To be raw.

To be real.

To be fucking human.

And guess what?

You're allowed to heal in a way that makes no sense to anyone but you. If your healing includes rage journaling, ice cream, loud music, or calling people out on their sh*t? Go off.

If it means quiet mornings, long walks, and therapy sessions that leave you emotionally hungover?

Do it.

If it means burning the fucking "nice girl" costume and owning your scars out loud?

Welcome home.

From One Crazy Bitch to Another

Listen… I still have moments. I still snap at stupid shit. I still cry in the car on the way to work sometimes. I still sometimes look in the mirror and ask, "Who the fuck even am I?"

But here's the difference now:

I know those moments don't define me.

I know I'm not broken.

I'm not unstable.

I'm not weak.

I'm healing And healing doesn't always look like peace and quiet. Sometimes it looks like rage and revolution.Sometimes it looks like standing in front of the girl who started the rumour and thinking: "Hoover this, bitch—I made it."

Final Truth Bomb for Chapter 1:

You don't owe anyone your silence.

You don't owe anyone your shame.

You don't owe anyone the version of yourself that made them comfortable.

You owe yourself the truth.

And the truth is this:

You are not who they say you are.

You never were.

You are WORTHY AS FUCK.

Now say it back to me…

I am worthy as fuck.

CHAPTER 2
The Relationship That Broke Me (So I Could Rebuild Me)

"He didn't ruin me. He revealed where I needed to Heal"

Out with the old… and into the fucking fire.

No one warns you that your first real relationship might not be the love story you dreamed of…It might be the unraveling of your entire damn identity. They don't tell you that butterflies can feel a lot like anxiety. They don't tell you the high of the honeymoon phase can become your drug of choice. They don't tell you that "I love you" can sound an awful lot like manipulation when you're starved for affection.

We all start with the same story:
Boy meets girl.
Boy likes girl.
Girl falls fast.
Shit gets messy.
Mine? Was textbook.
The first phone calls that made your stomach flip. The kisses that made you think this might be it. The moments where you start picturing your last name next to his on a mailbox somewhere down the line.
He met my friends.
He met my family.
He met the girl I was before the chaos cracked her open.

I thought I had won the damn lottery.
Until I found out the "once upon a time" had barely ended with someone else. Three-year relationship. Recently broken up.
And suddenly, I wasn't the main character.
I was the fucking rebound from the last chapter he couldn't close properly. But he had a story ready for that too: "It was already over before it ended." "She doesn't mean anything to me anymore." "You're the one I want." And I—being the loyal, hopeful, slightly naive version of me—believed him.

But here's the thing about gut instincts: They don't go away just because you want them to. They get louder. They tap your shoulder at 2am. They whisper, "Girl, something's off," right before the shit hits the fan. And eventually? They scream.

The Birth of the "Crazy" Girlfriend

It didn't happen all at once. First, it was how he always seemed a little too quiet after he got off the phone.
How he started calling me "paranoid" when I asked simple questions.
Then it was my fault.
My insecurity.
My imagination.
I didn't realize it at the time, but this was the beginning of my transformation—not into a woman in love, but into the girlfriend I swore I'd never be.
You know the one.
The one who checks your phone when you're in the shower. The one who memorizes license plates outside your house. The one who becomes a full-blown FBI agent with better intuition than a psychic hotline. I became her. I showed up at bars unannounced. I'd call just to "check in" and spiral if he didn't answer. And when he said he was going to a strip club with the boys? I fucking followed him there.

Yup. Full glam. Full drama. Sex and the City meets CIA sting operation He didn't know what hit him. I didn't sneak in quietly either. I walked in like I owned the damn place. Let's be clear: this wasn't confidence It was chaos in heels. I needed to see him. I needed him to see me. Because that's what happens when your nervous system stops feeling safe—
you trade in your inner peace for power plays.

And you call it love.

Make-Up Sex Is Not a Fucking Apology

Here's where it gets even messier. We fought like enemies. We made up like addicts.
And the sex? Oh, girl.did we have it wrong
We thought we were connecting.
We thought we were healing.
We thought it was intimacy.
It was a band-aid on a bullet wound. The passion wasn't love. It was survival. It was:
"Don't leave me."
"Prove you still want me."
"Let's pretend we're okay for one more night."
That kind of sex doesn't come with closeness. It comes with collapse. It's the moment your body confuses dopamine with devotion. And we wonder why we stay in toxic shit for years… Because even chaos can feel like home when that's what you've been trained to chase. The Signs Were There…
 But So Was I
The signs were never subtle. CDs with love songs would show up in his car—not from me. Anonymous notes. Messages I "wasn't supposed to see."
And even when I confronted him, even when the lies were obvious, I stayed. Because I didn't want to be the girl who gave up. Because I didn't want to lose. Because I thought I could love him into being a better man.
Spoiler alert:
You can't fix a man with your love. You'll just bleed yourself dry trying. I was obsessed. Possessed. Consumed. I knew every excuse. I had a sixth sense for every lie. And still—I stayed.

The Night I Lost Myself

One night, I was sick as hell—fever, sore throat, the whole dramatic rom-com setup where the boyfriend brings soup and rubs your back.

Except this wasn't a movie.

It was real life.

And he said, "I'm still going out."

I begged him to stay. He didn't. Hours passed. Then it was midnight. Then 2 a.m. Then 3 a.m. No phone call. No text. Just silence.

This was before smartphones. Before "Find My iPhone." All I had was a landline and a best friend with a full tank of gas. So we did what any woman on the edge of a full psychotic break does…

We fucking hunted.

We found out where he was—

his ex's best friend's house. With his ex-girlfriend I didn't cry. I didn't scream. I knocked on the goddamn door. And when he came outside? I stood there. In full heartbreak. Sick. Sweaty. Shaking. I didn't have words. I just had this look that said: "You have officially broken me."

The Fallout: When Rock Bottom Becomes a Crater

He dumped me the next week.

Said I was "too much."

Said I was controlling.

Said I needed help.

And what did he do? He went back to his ex. Publicly. Loudly. Like I never existed.

And I? I spiraled.

I cried until my throat hurt.

I stopped eating.

I couldn't sleep.

One night, I snapped. I drove to his house. Threw a bottle of pills on the ground in front of him—not to take them, but to make him see the damage. I didn't want to die. I

wanted someone to notice I was drowning. It wasn't a cry for attention.
It was a cry for rescue. But there's a problem with that: When you make someone else your lifeboat, you forget how to swim.

The Real Recovery Didn't Start with Closure
He didn't come running after me.
There was no apology.
No last-minute redemption arc. just silence. And that silence was the loudest fucking wake-up call of my life. For a while, I was humiliated. I kept asking myself: How the hell did I let it get that bad? But that question didn't help. It just made me feel worse.
The better question?
What was I trying to prove? To him. To myself. To the world. That I was lovable? That I could "win" him? That I could make him choose me over the girl he kept going back to?
Yeah… no.
That wasn't love. That was war. And I had to learn that just because something feels intense… doesn't mean it's meant for you.

Welcome to Withdrawal: Love as an Addiction
Let's talk science for a second.
(Yes, babe. Nerd moment incoming.)
When you're in a toxic relationship, your brain gets hooked on a cocktail of chaos: Dopamine from the highs Cortisol from the stress Oxytocin from the sex Adrenaline from the arguments It's a fucked-up Neuro-chemical soup—and your body learns to crave it.

So, when it's gone? You don't just miss the person. You go through withdrawal.
The same way an addict does.

You want to text them.
Check their socials.
Drive by their house.
Imagine wild-ass revenge scenarios while you cry in the bathtub listening to sad girl playlists. And if you're not careful, you'll mistake that craving for love. But baby, that's not love. That's emotional addiction. And it's time to detox.

The Work Begins (Spoiler: It's Not Cute)
The healing journey was ugly.
It didn't look like yoga mats, green smoothies, and crystals.
It looked like: Crying in my car before work. Writing unsent letters just to get the poison out. Blocking and unblocking his number 46 times. Letting my mom hold me while I sobbed like a toddler.
It looked like rage.
Like grief.
Like shame.
But somewhere in the wreckage…
I found something.
Me.
Not the version of me who tried to be "the cool girlfriend." Not the one who pretended she was fine while dying inside. Not the one who begged to be loved. The real me. And fuck, she was powerful.

Rebuilding After Ruin
I wish I could tell you there was one magical day where everything clicked.
There wasn't.
There were a thousand tiny moments. Moments where I chose myself instead of chasing him.
Moments where I stopped blaming myself for his fuckery.
Moments where I realized that being "too much" just meant I was too real for someone fake.
I rebuilt my confidence one broken belief at a time.

I stopped apologizing for having feelings.

I started asking myself, "What would a woman who knows her worth do right now?"

I realized I'd rather be alone than be someone's fucking emotional crutch. And slowly…

The chaos stopped feeling like home. The silence started feeling like peace.

And love?

It started looking a lot more like me.

For the Girl Still in It…

If you're still in that relationship—the one that keeps you guessing, keeps you shrinking, keeps you questioning your fucking sanity…

Here's what I want you to hear:

You're not broken.

You're not crazy.

You're not "too much."

You're just trying to survive a love that was never meant to be yours.

And I know you want to believe they'll change.

That if you just do this one more thing, they'll finally see your worth. But they won't. Because it's not about you. It's about them. Their wounds. Their fears. Their refusal to rise.

Don't let someone's refusal to heal be the reason you stay small. You've already lost enough time. You don't need to lose yourself too.

The Red Flags You Ignored (And What They Really Meant)

Let's just drag these out into the daylight, shall we?

Here are the flags I ignored:

He kept his phone on silent, face down. (Reference to todays red flags)

He got "defensive" every time I asked a simple question.

His ex was always somehow still around.
He said, "You're crazy" more times than he said, "I'm sorry."
I had to change to keep the peace.
And what they really meant?
He didn't respect me.
He needed control.
He wanted attention, not accountability.
He didn't love me.
He loved the power.
Read that again.
Worth Doesn't Beg
Let me hit you with the most important lesson:
Your worth is not negotiable.
It doesn't rise and fall with someone else's opinion. It doesn't shrink because someone couldn't see it. It's there loud and bold and radiant as fuck. And when you finally stop begging for crumbs? You start feasting on your own damn magic. That's when life gets delicious.

My Final Words on This Chapter (and Maybe Yours)

You might still be in it. You might still be unraveling. You might be staring at your phone, hoping he texts back.
Let me say this to the version of you that's scared to let go:
You are not meant to stay small to make someone else comfortable.
You are not here to earn love through suffering.
You are not broken—you're breaking free.
The girl I was back then thought her life was over when he walked away. But the woman I am now? She knows that moment was the beginning.
Of clarity.
Of fire.
Of fucking freedom.
So, if you're standing at your own emotional crossroads right now?
Choose you.

Not the you he wanted.
Not the you you had to become to keep the peace.
The real you.
She's been waiting.
And oh baby—she's a fucking gem.

I am worthy as fuck.

Chapter 3
Shattered Crowns & Fake Kings

"They wanted a trophy wife. I gave them a fucking revolution"

Let's get something straight:
There's no fucking shame in wanting love. There's no shame in dreaming about the white dress, the vows, the home, the family, the goddamn matching monogrammed towels. There's no shame in wanting to believe that "forever" means something when it comes out of someone's mouth.

But the shame creeps in when you wake up one day and realize you've become a cardboard cutout of yourself just to be loved by someone who couldn't handle the 3D version of you.

This is the chapter where my fairy tale burned to the ground.
Where the wedding ring felt more like handcuffs.
Where I traded my crown for crumbs and called it commitment.

Let's fucking begin.

Once Upon a Trauma Response

Here's the plot twist they don't put in the rom coms:
Sometimes your "happily ever after" starts with a man you already broke up with.
I know.
I know.

But the first lie we tell ourselves is that "maybe this time will be different."
That they've changed. That we've changed. That the chaos was just a phase. And when he came back,
I believed it.

The same man who had ghosted me emotionally, betrayed my trust, left me a nervous system in human form—he showed up with that sad-boy face, a promise of change, and a speech that could've won a fucking Oscar.

And I... let him back in.

Because sometimes the wound looks more familiar than the healing.

The Engagement That Looked Like a Movie Scene (But Felt Like a Performance)

We fell back into each other fast.
Too fast. It was butterflies mixed with a fire alarm.
Hot and dangerous. But I was determined to make it work.

We moved in together. Started playing house And one day—boom—he proposed.
Publicly.
Dramatically.
With people watching, clapping, taking photos like, we were the fucking royal couple.

And I said yes.

Because in that moment, I wasn't thinking about all the nights I'd cried myself to sleep.
I was thinking about the fairytale.
About proving that the story wasn't over. That love could win. That maybe I wasn't as broken as I felt.
Spoiler alert:
Love doesn't win when one person is playing a role and the other is writing the damn script.

The Pre-Wedding Breakdown No One Talks About

Two weeks before the wedding—my body screamed at me. Anxiety. Insomnia. Nausea. I was spiralling like a damn tornado in a bridal shop I called my mom. I called friends. I told everyone:
"I think I'm making a mistake."
And you know what they said?
"Cold feet is normal."
"You're just nervous."
"You love him. You'll be fine."

So I ignored the sirens.
I shoved the truth back down.
And I walked down that aisle like a goddamn soldier heading into battle dressed in white lace and fake hope.

Let me tell you—nothing hurts quite like smiling through a ceremony when your gut is screaming, **"RUN."**

From Wife to "Why Do You Look Like That?"

For a hot second, I was happy. Married life had its glow. We got a house. We bought furniture. We threw parties. I made his lunches, and he kissed my forehead on the way to work.
The Pinterest version of us looked perfect.

But perfection has a short shelf life when it's built on shaky ass foundations.

The cracks started slow. The first was a night out that turned into him being driven home by another woman. A woman who had kissed him in her car… in our fucking driveway.

The betrayal wasn't even subtle—it was bold. Disrespectful. Public.

And when I confronted him?

He told me it "meant nothing."
Like I was supposed to be relieved that the kiss in our driveway wasn't meaningful cheating—it was casual cheating.

Fuck. That.

Then came the comments:

"You're wearing that?"
"Didn't you used to do your hair more?"
"You've put on a bit of weight, haven't you?"

It wasn't about love anymore.
It was about image,About control,About shrinking me into something more... palatable.
The Trophy Wife Setup
Here's what I eventually realized:

He didn't want a wife.
He wanted a fucking mascot.

Someone who could stand beside him in photos.
Smile on cue, Stay small, stay pretty, stay quiet, and I was cracking under the pressure.

The "happy weight" from our first year of marriage? Suddenly a problem.,the messy bun I wore around the house? Suddenly "unattractive. The comfort I thought I could finally exhale into? Gone.

He wanted the woman he married to stay frozen in time. *Like a Barbie still in the box.*

But newsflash:
I'm not plastic.
I evolve.
And I sure as hell wasn't put here to be a prop in someone else's performance.

The Night That Fucked Me Up Forever
Then came the threesome. Yep. You read that right.
He suggested it. Said it was "just a fantasy."
Said it would spice things up.
I said no.
Then I said maybe. Then I said yes—because deep down, I thought if I could become his fantasy, maybe he'd stop looking elsewhere for it. We set boundaries, he crossed them. I cried; he didn't stop.

I sat in the next room while it happened. tears running down my face. feeling smaller than I ever had before That night, something in me died the little girl who believed in love,The woman who still hoped for change,The wife who thought she could make it work.
Gone.
Let's talk about the part no one warns you about…The part where you're not only grieving the loss of a marriage— you're grieving the version of yourself that thought this was love. You're grieving the woman who thought she found forever,The woman who held on even when her hands were bleeding.

The woman who thought that if she was just "enough," he'd stay.
And the worst part?
You have to grieve that woman while growing a human inside of you I used to stare at the bathroom mirror, belly growing, tears burning like acid in my eyes, asking myself the same question on a loop:

"How the fuck did I get here?"

I wasn't dumb.
I wasn't weak.
I wasn't naïve.

But I was conditioned—to believe love meant sacrifice, meant silence, meant surviving shit that should've been dealbreakers. I was taught to "keep the family together," "give it time," "don't air your dirty laundry," and all that toxic, patriarchal bullshit that keeps women stuck in pretty cages.

I was loyal to a man who wouldn't even answer his phone when I was cramping and spotting.
I was committed to a marriage that was already emotionally divorced.
I was carrying his child while he was creating a life with someone else.

And still—I blamed me.
My body.
My attitude.
My independence.
My inability to shut the fuck up and smile through it.

I thought: Maybe if I was less... me?

Less loud.
Less opinionated.
Less hormonal.
Less tired from 6 a.m. shifts and 10 p.m. tears.

But fuck that.
The Silent Strength of Single Motherhood

When you become a single mom while still married, there's a unique kind of grief that hits. It's not just the absence of a partner—it's the presence of betrayal. You sit in OB appointments alone.
You fill out forms that say "married" but feel like a damn lie. You register for baby gifts with no clue how you're going to afford anything.

And still—you survive.

You fold the baby clothes.
You build the crib.
You paint the nursery with your mother.
You work double shifts, rub your own swollen feet, and cry quietly into the freezer when the cravings won't quit and no one is there to rub your back.

You become your own village.
And the strength you find in that?
Unreal.

He missed every milestone.
Every kick, every late-night craving, every emotional breakdown over which breast pump to buy.

But I didn't.

I was there.
And that's what fucking matters.

The Baby Came... And So Did the Fire

When she arrived, I expected to crumble.

I thought I'd be too broken, too exhausted, too bitter to feel joy.
But instead—I felt fire.

Holding her wasn't just love. It was a resurrection.
It was the moment I stopped asking, "Why me?" and started saying "Watch me."

I wasn't just a mom; I was a mother fucking warrior.

Her cry didn't scare me—it grounded me.
Her tiny hands gave me a reason to let go of the big disappointments.
Her heartbeat regulated mine.

She saved me.
And she'll never have to.
Because I will never let her grow up thinking love should feel like waiting by the door.

The Glow-Up: Not Just a TikTok Trend
Postpartum was hell.
But that glow-up?
It was earned.

I didn't bounce back—I clawed back.

From the wreckage.
From the lies.
From the feeling that I'd never be wanted again.

I found therapy.
I found boundaries.
I found self-respect hidden under a pile of old wedding photos and court documents.

I got my license renewed and my name changed back. I stopped flinching every time my phone lit up. I deleted the texts I used to reread for signs of love. I finally wore shorts again—stretch marks and all.

And when people whispered, "She's changed…"

Damn right I did.
I became the version of me who doesn't beg to be chosen.
I choose myself now.

If You're Still In It—This Part's for You

If you're sitting in the ashes right now If you're still crying in your minivan in the driveway while pretending everything is fine… If you're still asking, "What did I do wrong?" when deep down, you know you were always too much woman for a small-ass man…

Here's what I want you to know:

You are not broken.
You are not unlovable.
You are not too much.

You were just wearing your crown in the wrong kingdom.
You are not a supporting actress in someone else's redemption arc.

You are the fucking main character.

The Worthy AF Reality

When people ask how I "moved on," I don't say time healed it.
Time doesn't heal sh*t, it makes more bearable

Truth does.

Owning your story.
Owning your worth.
Owning the moments you stayed when you should've run—and forgiving the fuck out of yourself for it.

Healing isn't pretty.
It's ugly crying on bathroom floors.
It's voice notes to your best friend at 3 a.m. that sound like therapy and tequila all at once. It's deleting his number and forgetting it, then remembering it again in a nightmare.

But eventually?

You stop waking up wishing you were someone else.
You stop apologizing for your strength.
You stop needing closure—and become your own fucking completion.

Final Thought Before We Flip the Page

If he left you broken, don't stay there. If he called you too loud, too needy, too much—turn that volume the fuck UP. If you loved him harder than you loved yourself—it's time to change that ratio.

This chapter wasn't about the man who left.It's about the woman who rose.You don't need a partner to be complete.

You need truth, fire, and a whole lot of unlearning.

You are not just a survivor. You are the rebirth.
Your crown isn't shattered.
It's reforged.

Stronger. Heavier. And this time—no fake kings allowed.

I am worthy as fuck.

Chapter 4: The Silent Shame of a 'Broken' Body

"Infertility made me question my worth-but it also made me fight for it"

The Unspoken Struggle

Let's rewind to 2006, there was no Instagram. No gender reveals confetti cannons. No Facebook "We're Expecting!" announcements with matching ultrasound selfies. There were definitely no online support groups or TikToks about hormone injections or PCOS-friendly diets.

Back then, infertility was a whispered topic, cloaked in shame and silence. Support groups were scarce, and the few that existed were often inaccessible or unknown to many.

So, when my journey began, I didn't have a sisterhood. I had Google and a fragile hope that maybe this time, my body wouldn't betray me.

Hormones, Hope, and a Hell of a Drive

For four fucking years, my life revolved around syringes, hormone surges, and early morning drives—not across town, but an hour and a half away to another damn city. Every month, like clockwork, I'd drive in for bloodwork at dawn and ultrasounds to check my eggs. And if my follicles weren't the right size?

Tough shit.

Better luck next cycle.

And then there was his sperm. Yes, we had to wrap his little swimmers in tin foil to keep them warm like some sad science fair project. You ever drive down the highway praying your man's sperm doesn't die in your lap? That's a special kind of stress.

Every month, I was hopeful. Every month, I was devastated.

And every single fucking time someone around me got pregnant "accidentally,"

I wanted to scream. I wasn't angry at them—but I was angry. Angry at the universe. At my body. At whatever "plan" God supposedly had. I remember whispering, Why not me? over and over again like it was a broken prayer.

People said things like

It'll happen when you least expect it" or "

God only gives you what you can handle."

And if I had a dollar for every time someone said *"Just stop trying so hard"*—

I could've funded my own damn fertility clinic.

Sex Becomes a Science Experiment

At one point, sex stopped being fun and started being… scheduled. It wasn't about desire anymore—it was about ovulation windows and cervical mucus. If you've never had your marriage reduced to "Can you get hard in the next ten minutes or we're gonna miss the fertility window?"—count your fucking blessings.

The romance was gone.

The spontaneity was dead.

And we were exhausted.

I was pumping my body full of hormones that made me cry at dog food commercials and gain weight like I was training for a sumo match. My skin broke out, my clothes stopped fitting, and I didn't recognize the woman in the mirror.

I felt broken.

The Miracle… and the Madness

Eventually, after six or seven rounds of IUI, I decided I needed a break. No more needles. No more tin-foiled sperm. I needed to breathe.

And then—boom. I got pregnant.

I was playing in a baseball tournament when it happened. I hadn't had a period in a while, but I chalked it up to my body still being all jacked up from the meds. A friend convinced me to take a test she had lying around, and holy shit—it was positive.

I was two and a half months pregnant.

It was this weird cocktail of

shock,

joy,

and disbelief.

After everything—everything—my body had done it. She had held on. And for a minute, I was on top of the fucking world, But that didn't last long. At four months pregnant, I left my marriage.

Leaving While Growing Life

Leaving a man is hard.

Leaving while pregnant—when your hormones are wild and your whole identity feels like it's unraveling—is soul-crushing.

We had been together seven years. Married for five. We had our routines—our shows, our dinner habits, our shared toothbrush drawer. And then suddenly, it was just me. And the baby.

I didn't even know who I was anymore. I felt like a ghost inside my own life.

And the kicker?

He was supportive during the pregnancy.

He came to appointments.

He showed up.

He might've been a shitty husband—but he always wanted to be a dad.

And I let him.

Because no matter what happened between us, I wasn't going to be the reason my daughter didn't have both of her parents cheering her on at basketball games or clapping for her at school plays. That was my choice—to co-parent with grace. And whether I liked it or not, the woman he got pregnant while I was four months along… well, her baby was going to be my daughter's sibling.

And that shit… that's a pill you don't just swallow—you choke on it.

Two Pregnancies. One Truth.

When I found out about her pregnancy—confirmed by an anonymous call at work—I broke. Not a cute cry. A fetal-position-on-the-bathroom-floor kind of breakdown. I was still pregnant. Still carrying our baby. Still recovering from years of hormone trauma and emotional warfare. And he was already playing house with someone new.

It didn't just hurt. It annihilated me.

My mind told me I wasn't enough. My body told me I was barely holding it together. And society? Society told me to be graceful, not bitter. To smile and forgive and "be the bigger person."

Fuck that.

I allowed the grief to come. I screamed in my car. I punched pillows. I cried until I couldn't see. And slowly, one breath at a time, I realized something:

This wasn't about her. It wasn't even about him. It was about me reclaiming me. Rebuilding From the Rubble

I became a mother on my own terms. And that little girl? She was the miracle I wasn't supposed to have.

Yes, I lived with my parents. Yes, I had days where I didn't get out of bed. Yes, I had moments where I begged him to take me back—because that's what grief and trauma do.

But I didn't stay there.

I began rebuilding.

Fiercely.

Clumsily.

Imperfectly.

I asked for help.

I went to therapy.

I started speaking my truth—even when it made people uncomfortable.

Because no one talks about the loneliness of pregnancy after betrayal.

No one talks about the rage that comes when you see other couples celebrating gender reveals while you're unpacking your stuff in your childhood bedroom with a baby in your belly.

No one talks about how fucking brave it is to still choose joy, to still choose life, when everything you planned has burned to ash.

But that's exactly what I did.

My Realization

Infertility broke me open. It tore down everything I thought I knew about being a woman, a wife, a partner, a mother.

But it also made space.

Space for a new kind of strength. One that didn't need validation from a husband. One that didn't shrink for the comfort of others. One that didn't tie her worth to her fertility, her marriage, or the size of her jeans.

I realized that my self-worth never left me. It had just been buried under hormone injections, broken promises, and other people's bullshit.

My Advice to You

If you're walking this road—through infertility, heartbreak, betrayal, or all three—

Here's what I want you to know:

You are not broken.

You are not a failure.

You are not too emotional, too dramatic, too sensitive.

You are fucking human.

You are allowed to scream. To rage. To grieve. And also—to laugh. To heal. To rise again.

Fuck the fairy tale.

Build your own story. Because what's waiting on the other side of your pain? Is power.

And if you're still in it? That's okay too.

This chapter isn't the end. It's the beginning.

You are the miracle.

You are the fire.

You are worthy as fuck.

The Body That Betrayed Me… Or Did It?

For years, I looked at my body like it had failed me.

Like it had one job—and fucked it up spectacularly.

I hated my hormones, I hated my bloating, I hated the weight gain, the stretch marks, the skin that no longer glowed.

I hated how I couldn't control any of it.

Infertility doesn't just mess with your ovaries—it hijacks your identity, every negative pregnancy test felt like a rejection letter from womanhood, and when I finally did get pregnant, I felt like I wasn't allowed to be anything but grateful. Grateful, even when I was puking in my car. Grateful, even when I cried at commercials. Grateful, even when I was alone.

You know what we don't talk about enough?

That you can be grateful for your pregnancy and still be grieving the version of you that got lost along the way,I was pregnant.,and I was heartbroken,and I didn't know that both could be true.

No one teaches you how to hold space for joy and rage at the same time.

But I had to learn.

Because my daughter deserved a mom who wasn't pretending to be okay.

She deserved a mom who actually was okay.

And that meant I had to stop pretending my pain didn't exist just because I finally got what I wanted.

I had to stop punishing my body for what it didn't do and start honouring it for what it survived.

This body?
She held on.
She carried life.

She walked out of betrayal, pregnant and alone, and still showed up.

That's not broken.

That's badass.

Unpacking the Guilt

But let's talk about the real mind fuck: the guilt, the guilt of getting pregnant after years of trying—when so many women still hadn't, the guilt of not feeling happy every day, the guilt of secretly wishing the father of your child would magically become the man he pretended to be, the guilt of still loving someone who hurt you.

We talk a lot about physical symptoms during pregnancy.

But no one talks about the emotional tornado that comes when your future implodes mid-trimester.

I wasn't just mourning the marriage—I was mourning the fantasy.

The version of my life I built in my head.

The matching family pajamas.

The Christmas photos with coordinated outfits.

The Sunday mornings with pancakes and cartoons and love that didn't leave, instead, I got court dates and custody schedules, and a birth plan I wrote alone.

But here's the plot twist no one saw coming:

The life I built after all that.

It was fucking better, not because it was perfect.

But because it was mine.

Owning My Messy Middle

There's this part of healing that no one wants to post about. The in-between. The messy middle. When you're not shattered anymore, but you're still fragile, when you're functional, but still flinch at baby showers, when you've accepted what happened, but there's still a tiny part of you that wants an apology that will never come.

That's the space I lived in for a while.

Going to work.
Growing a human.
Going to therapy.
Grieving what could've been.

Trying to believe in what could still be.

It was quiet.
It was exhausting.
And it was sacred.

Because that's where I became her.

Not the version of me that had it all figured out.
But the version of me that was real.
Raw.
Resilient as hell.
The version that didn't need a man to validate her.
The version that stopped making herself small to keep the peace, the version that knew her worth—even when her world had fallen apart.
That's when I stopped waiting to be saved.
And started saving my damn self.

Your Body Isn't the Problem

Here's the thing I wish someone had screamed in my face back then:

Your body is not the problem.

Your body is trying.

Even when you hate her.

Even when you talk shit about her.

Even when you ignore her needs and compare her to every filtered, fertile woman on your feed.

She is still trying.

She's not the enemy.

She's the battlefield.

And sis, she's been fighting for you even when you weren't fighting for her.

So, give her a little grace.

She's been through hell and back.
She deserves your kindness.
She deserves your forgiveness.
She deserves to feel like home again.

Not a war zone.

You Don't Have to Be Grateful All the Time

Can we just kill this toxic positivity bullshit for a second?, You don't have to be grateful all the time, you don't have to whisper "at least I got pregnant" to make people comfortable with your story, you don't have to sugarcoat your pain to be worthy of support.

Your grief is real.
Your rage is real.
Your exhaustion is real.

And you're allowed to feel all of it.

You're allowed to scream into your pillow and still show up for your baby shower, you're allowed to cry on the way to the OB office and still be excited to hear the heartbeat, you're allowed to be a walking contradiction.

Because healing isn't linear.

And gratitude doesn't cancel out grief.

Co-Parenting with Someone Who Broke You

Let's just call it what it is: co-parenting with the person who broke your fucking heart is a masterclass in emotional regulation. There's nothing like handing your baby over for the weekend to the man who gaslit you, cheated on you, and made you feel like you weren't enough.

It's hard.

It's not "mature" or "noble" or "brave."

It's survival.

But I made a decision early on: I wasn't going to let my pain poison my daughter's view of her dad. Even if I wanted to, even if I had every reason to.

Because she didn't ask for this.

And she deserved peace—even if I had to choke down every bitter word to give it to her. Was it easy? Hell no. Did I do it perfectly? Also no.

But I did it.

And now, years later, my daughter knows she is loved by both of her parents, she knows I never used her as a pawn, she knows I never made her carry the weight of our mistakes.

And that's the real win.

The Truth About "Bouncing Back"

Spoiler alert: I didn't bounce back.

I crawled forward.

Some days I stood tall.

Some days I face planted.

Some days I wore the same leggings for 72 hours and cried into my cereal.

But I kept going.

Not because I'm superhuman.

Not because I'm stronger than you.

But because I had to.

Because there was a tiny girl watching me.

And I knew that if I wanted her to know her worth…

I had to remember mine.

Even if I was relearning it one shaky step at a time.

You Are Not Alone

If you're reading this while holding a negative test… or a baby, you never thought you'd have… or a broken heart from the person who helped you make them—

I see you.

You are not alone.
You are not invisible.
You are not unworthy.

You are navigating one of the hardest fucking things a woman can go through, and you're doing it with more grace and guts than anyone knows.

So, whether your mid-cycle, mid-divorce, mid-breakdown, or mid-rebuild—

This chapter is for you.

Not to give you hope wrapped in a bow.

But to remind you that you're still here.
Still breathing.
Still fighting.
Still capable of becoming someone even stronger on the other side of this pain.

Let's Be Fucking Clear

Infertility didn't ruin me, It rewired me, It showed me who I was when everything I thought defined me was stripped away.

And what was left?

A woman who doesn't beg, A woman who doesn't shrink, A woman who doesn't accept crumbs from men who feast elsewhere, A woman who may not have a fairy tale—

but has a fucking legacy.

Because I didn't just survive infertility.

I used it to become the most powerful version of myself.

And now?

I am worthy as fuck.

Chapter 5: Nice Guys, Red Flags, and Red Wine

"Healing didn't come from-it came from losing myself and clawing my back"

Why I Thought a Good Orgasm Could Heal Me (Plot Twist: It Couldn't)

Let's talk about the aftermath.

Not the cute, color-coded "healing era" where you're sipping green juice and doing sunrise yoga with your third eye open. I mean the real aftermath.

The "crying on your kitchen floor at 2 a.m. while spooning cheesecake into your mouth with your bare hand" kind of aftermath.

The "faking a smile in the grocery store while silently debating whether to throat-punch someone who says 'everything happens for a reason'" kind.

That aftermath.

When the dust settles after your life implodes and you're left standing there in sweatpants that haven't been washed in 12 days, holding a baby in one hand and your shattered identity in the other.

That was me.

My daughter was nine months old, I had just moved back into the house that used to be ours, the house that once smelled like his cologne and stupid man-body wash, Now it smelled like baby formula, stress sweat, and desperation with a hint of Glade plug-in.

He had officially moved in with his new girlfriend, And I was navigating the chaotic mind fuck that is single motherhood and "what the fuck do I do now?"

I didn't know who I was anymore.

I knew how to pack a diaper bag like a boss.

I knew how to fake a smile at work.

I knew how to fold laundry while crying and whisper-singing lullabies through gritted teeth.

But me?

She was gone.

And yet… weekends saved me.

He took our daughter every weekend—and at first, that shattered me, I felt like a bad mom for needing the break, for enjoying it, for breathing when she was gone.

But then I realized something…

Those weekends were my lifeline, They were the first taste of freedom I'd had in years.

And honey—freedom is a dangerous drug.

Enter: The Red Wine Era

I started going out again.

Not "hot girl summer" going out—more like "put on clean leggings and drink sangria on a patio with my girls while we talk shit about our exes" going out.

I remembered how to laugh.

I remembered how to flirt.

I remembered what it felt like to feel seen by someone—anyone—other than a toddler and a co-worker who kept asking if I was okay because I looked "tired."

Spoiler alert: I wasn't tired. I was fucking exhausted.

And yeah… I started dating again.

Because I thought I was healed.

(Spoiler alert: I wasn't. I was just angry, horny, and craving dopamine.)

I thought healing meant:

Never crying over a man again.

Never being the girl who double-texts.

Never being the dumb bitch who believes the lies.

But if I'm being honest?

That version of healing was just trauma with a push-up bra and an extra glass of cab sauv.

Meet the Nice Guy

After all the chaos, the betrayal, the lies—I told the universe I wanted something different.

And like Amazon Prime with 24-hour delivery, he showed up.

The Nice Guy.

Tall. Sweet. Educated.

Held a real job. Used actual grammar. Took interest in my day. Remembered my kid's name, He even brought groceries over when I was sick., I mean, seriously—this man folded my fucking laundry without being asked.

And yet... something didn't click.

Now, before you get all judgy and write me off as a shallow bitch, hear me out, this guy was the human equivalent of warm soup and fuzzy socks.

Safe. Comforting. Good for you.

But you know when you've been on a diet, and you're craving a damn Snickers bar, and you know the right choice is the sad-ass carrots in your fridge?

Yeah. He was the carrots.

I wanted to want him. I really did.

But I was still addicted to the chaos, the highs and lows, the "will he text back?" emotional rollercoaster I'd mistaken for passion.

Nice guys don't play mind games.

They don't withhold love.

They don't make you chase.

And I didn't know what the fuck to do with that.

I Was the Red Flag

Let's get brutally honest, I was the walking red flag.

I Only replied when I felt like it Ghosted him after a great date, picked fights out of boredom, gave him just enough attention to keep him around, but not enough to build anything real

Why?

Because I didn't know how to receive healthy love, It felt foreign. Uncomfortable. Like wearing heels two sizes too small—you're supposed to look good, but inside you're screaming.

And yet... I kept seeing him.

Why?

Because the sex. Was. Fucking. Fire.

I expected it to be mild, like mashed potatoes without salt, But no—this man brought Thanksgiving dinner with all the sides and a damn encore.

He didn't flop over and snore after two minutes.

He didn't act like foreplay was optional.

He didn't need a damn instruction manual.

And for the first time in years, I felt... desired. Worshipped.

But even that couldn't mask the truth:

I didn't love him.

I loved the idea of him.

And that, my friend, is a dangerous illusion.

The Almost Proposal

One night, over a dinner he made from scratch, this man—this actual unicorn—looked me in the eye and said:

"You don't have to do this alone, You don't need to work yourself to death, I'll take care of you and your daughter. I want to."

And my entire nervous system short-circuited.

Because this wasn't just "nice."

This was provider energy.

The kind of offer half the internet says we should be manifesting.

And you know what I felt?

Panic.

Rage.

Trapped.

Like I was being offered a gilded cage.

Sure, it was beautiful. Soft. Comfortable.

But it was still a fucking cage, Because I had just gotten out of one, I had just spent years having my worth measured by how much I could please, perform, and stay small, and now here he was—offering to

"save" me.

Even if his heart was in the right place, mine wasn't, So I sat there, staring at my plate of perfectly cooked salmon, blinking back tears, and I knew.

I had to let him go.

The Goodbye That Didn't Break Me

Letting go of a good man is a different kind of grief.

There was no betrayal, No screaming fights.

No slamming doors or shattered dishes, Just honesty.

I told him I couldn't give him what he deserved, That I wasn't healed, That I didn't want more kids—and I knew, deep down, he did.

Even if he said it didn't matter... it would have.

And I refused to be someone's second heartbreak.

So, I walked away.

It was sad.

But not for me

Because for once—I left before I lost myself, and a few years later, I saw him again, With his wife, And his son.

And guess what?

I smiled.

Not a fake smile, not a "I hope your new life sucks" smile, A real one, because he got what he always wanted, and so did I:

Myself.

The Realization (AKA: Me, the Bulldozer)

Here's the truth nobody posts in their healing montage:

I wasn't just recovering from being betrayed, I was recovering from betraying myself.

From ignoring red flags.

From chasing crumbs.

From staying small so someone else could feel big.

And when I met someone who actually treated me with care?

I bulldozed right through him.

I weaponized silence.

I dismissed kindness.

I mistook emotional safety for boredom.

I was the toxic one.

And instead of shaming myself for that, I started doing the one thing most people never do:

I took accountability.

I stopped blaming the ex.

I stopped saying "all men are the same."

I stopped choosing chaos and calling it chemistry.

And I started asking:

What does love feel like when it's healthy?

Answer:

It feels boring—at first, because your nervous system doesn't recognize peace as safe, it thinks the person who texts back right away is suspicious, and that's the unsexy truth of trauma; We crave what hurt us because we haven't learned to recognize what heals us.

So, What Happened Next?

I stayed single.

Not lonely.

Not bitter.

Not jaded.

Single.

And healing.

And whole.

I stopped looking for someone to save me, stopped confusing good dick with good love, stopped believing that if it wasn't dramatic, it wasn't real.

I redefined what I wanted.

Not a savior.

Not a sugar daddy.

Not a knight in emotional armour.

Just a real fucking human who could meet me in the mess, love me in the silence, and respect me even when I was wearing adult diapers on my period and eating popcorn for dinner.

But before I could meet him?

I had to become her.

The woman who didn't settle.

Who didn't chase, who didn't confuse consistency for weakness, The woman who knew she was already complete.

My Advice to You

If you're sitting there crying over the guy who seemed perfect "on paper" but didn't ignite your soul, That's okay. If you're choosing yourself even when it's lonely? *That's growth.* If you realize you were the red flag in your last relationship? *Welcome to radical fucking accountability.*

Here's what I know for sure:

You are allowed to grieve people you outgrew; you are allowed to walk away from someone good if it doesn't feel right, you are allowed to be single without being "in waiting" for a man.

Nice guys don't finish last.

They just finish with someone who's actually ready, and babe—when that day comes?

You won't sabotage it, you won't question it, you won't run from it.

Because you'll know:

You don't need to be saved; you just need to be seen.

And until then?

You'll be busy building your empire, kissing your own shoulders, raising babies, dreams, and standards, you'll be sipping your red wine, rolling your eyes at your past self, and whispering…

"Damn. Look at her now."

I am worthy as fuck.

CHAPTER 6: The Perception; You belong To Me

"It wasn't passion. It was possession dressed up in manipulation..A hostage situation"

I'll give you a second to breathe before we dive into this one.

Because if you've ever been stalked, controlled, or felt your safety shrink to the size of a locked bathroom door—you know this isn't just a story.

It's a fucking war story in heels.

And this chapter? It's for the women who survived it, And the ones who are still pretending they're "fine."

Let's rewind—back to the moment I thought I was just getting laid, after ending things with the Nice Guy—you know, the one who wanted to take care of me and fold my laundry—I was still raw, restless, and wearing my bad bitch mask like it actually fucking fit.

So, when I ran into this guy outside a lunch spot—someone I'd seen around, someone who had that look (you know the one: rough around the edges, a little smirk, probably owns a pair of handcuffs for reasons you don't ask about)—I gave him my number.

He wasn't jaw-dropping hot, but he had that energy, The "I could ruin your life but make it feel like a vacation" kind of energy, and after Nice Guy Smoothie Bowl, I wanted the steak tartare of bad decisions.

It started with a kiss.

One of those neck-grabbing, hair-twisting, melt-into-the-wall type kisses that erases logic faster than tequila. He came over to hang out, and we were watching a movie…

but let's be real—this wasn't Netflix and chill, this was Netflix and "take me now." He kissed me, slid his hand up the back of my neck, threaded his fingers into my hair—and BAM.

The horny feminist in me evaporated.

I wasn't a single mom folding baby laundry anymore—I was Cat woman in pleather, owning the night and the sex. I stood up, led him to my room, and let myself become someone I didn't recognize—but fuck, did I love her.

The next morning, I laid in bed thinking,

"Did that just happen?, I wasn't in love, I wasn't thinking long-term, But I was definitely thinking long… you get the idea.

Then came the text.

Not a "had a great time" or "you looked beautiful."

Nope, It was filthy, It was hot, It was the kind of message that makes you clench your thighs and look over your shoulder just reading it, Ladies—he had the audacity to talk to me like I was his personal fantasy, I had never had a man talk to me like this, to be honest I didn't even know how to respond. What I did know

I Was. Hooked.

We weren't dating, We weren't official, We were fucking. We were friends with benefits, and it was incredible, I'd call him after a night out, or when my daughter was at her dad's, It was my version of rebellion, It was the only thing that made me feel powerful when everything else in my life felt like drowning in formula bottles and divorce paperwork.

And he gave me the thing I couldn't buy anywhere:

That high.

The kind of high that doesn't just light up your body—it hijacks your entire nervous system and makes you forget what red flags even look like.

Until they started showing up, not red flags waving in the wind, No. These were more like quiet whispers under the surface, little things, like him getting moody if I didn't answer fast enough, Like the way he'd ask where I was before he asked how I was, like calling five, six, seven times in a row when I didn't pick up.

The first time he insulted me, I laughed, He said I was acting like a "spoiled bitch, I rolled my eyes, second time, He called me a stuffed pig, I froze. But I didn't block him, third time Gutter slut, And I wish I could say I walked away then.

But I didn't.

Because the sex was still good, Because the compliments still came after the cruelty, Because I wasn't ready to admit what I already knew.

The truth is—I was addicted.

Addicted to the way he touched me.

Addicted to the fantasy that I could control the chaos by managing his moods, addicted to the power I felt, this is probably the first time I learned what it meant to have no inhibitions. Addicted to the idea that if I just played it cool, I could have all the pleasure without the price.

Spoiler alert:

There's always a fucking price.

And mine came in the form of shattered boundaries, a dismantled identity, and eventually—a restraining order.

He started calling my work "just to say hi." He'd drive by my house at night and text me that he "missed my smile." The worst part is he didn't drive, ya so he had friends drive him around He'd show up uninvited and get angry when I wouldn't let him in.

Once, I picked up after ignoring 15 missed calls and he screamed, "You think you're too good for me now?"

I hung up.

And he kept calling, the calls would switch from rage to begging, from name-calling to -showering with me compliments and I am sorry's . I constantly reminded him this wasn't a relationship I didn't want that.

It was like dating Jekyll and Hyde—if both of them were horny, manipulative, and had access to my schedule, And the scariest part? I still let him come over sometimes.

Because saying "no" felt dangerous.

Because ignoring him felt like baiting a bomb.

Because trauma will trick you into thinking you're safer in the lion's den than outside of it.

So, I played the game.

Sometimes willingly, sometimes just to survive.

One night, he showed up at my house uninvited, I cracked the door, trying to avoid a scene, He pushed past me, sat on my couch, and refused to leave, When I said I was calling my dad, he grabbed my phone, pocketed it, and smirked like he'd won.

I sat on the floor.

He sat beside me.

Then he pinned me down—knees on my shoulders, hands holding mine, pressing me into the carpet.

I couldn't breathe.

Couldn't move.

Could barely speak.

He didn't hit me.

But that doesn't mean it wasn't violence, it was control, Domination, Terror wrapped in a man's smile.

Eventually, he got up. Left like nothing happened.

And I cried on the floor until the sun came up.

That was the night I realized:

This isn't sexy.

This isn't fun.

This isn't a game.

This is a fucking crime scene with perfume on.

The next morning, Children's Services knocked on my door.

Anonymous tip.

Questions about my daughter, they went through my home, my kitchen, my closets, they interviewed my daughter's father, they stripped my baby down and checked her body for signs of abuse.

And I broke.

Because I had protected the monster, I thought I was keeping my daughter safe by playing nice, playing quiet, playing along, But I had let him dictate the rules, And the game was over.

When Obsession Wears a Smile: The Aftermath

They say it takes a woman seven times to leave an abusive partner for good.

But they never talk about how many times it takes for her to believe she's allowed to.

After the Children's Services visit, I finally did what I should've done months earlier.

I told someone.

I told the truth.

The whole ugly, humiliating, soul-shattering truth, Not the sugarcoated version where I was still "in control" or "handling it.", No. I let it all fall out—every name he called me, every time I let him in when I was terrified, every threat, every bruise on my dignity that you couldn't see, And the moment I said it out loud, the mask cracked, I wasn't the strong girl anymore.

I was just a girl who didn't want to die.

I went to the police.

I brought them the voicemails, the texts, the call logs.

I showed them the bullet.

Yes. A fucking bullet, He had handed me three and said, "One for me, one for you, and one for whoever tries to stop me, I only kept one, People ask me why. Why keep something so triggering, Because I needed the reminder that this wasn't a dream.

That my trauma wasn't "just sex that got complicated.", It was real, and it nearly cost me everything.

He was arrested.

Charged with forcible confinement, uttering death threats, criminal harassment, and stalking.

A restraining order was issued.

No contact.

No proximity.

No loopholes.

I finally felt safe.

Until I didn't.

Blocked numbers started calling, Burner accounts sent me messages like:

"Drop the charges or it gets worse."

"You ruined his life. Now let's ruin yours."

"Hope you like being a single mom with no fucking job."

And they were from women.

Other girls.

His flying monkeys, Women he manipulated into thinking I was the villain, and he was the broken, misunderstood prince.

They threatened to beat me up, to take my kid, to show up at my job.

And the worst part?

I believed them.

Because I knew what he was capable of, Because I knew he wouldn't stop just because the law said he had to, because restraining orders are just paper—and he didn't respect boundaries printed in ink or spoken with shaking breath.

The police tried.

They really did.

Patrols would drive by my house, I'd call to report threats, and they'd say, "There's nothing we can do unless he shows up again."

So I lived in hyper-vigilance.

Curtains drawn.

Doors locked.

Panic every time the phone rang.

Fear when headlights passed my driveway at night.

I didn't feel like a badass anymore, I felt like a fucking prisoner in my own life, and here's the part no one tells you:

When you finally break free, you don't feel free.

You feel ashamed.

You feel like a statistic.

You hear the voice in your head whisper,

"How the fuck did I let this happen?"

You replay every red flag you ignored, you rehearse what you should've said, you beat yourself up for being scared, for being addicted to the high, for believing the lies, and people around you—well, they ask all the wrong fucking questions.

"Why didn't you leave sooner?"

"Why didn't you block him?"

"Why didn't you tell anyone?"

Let me tell you something:

Fear rewrites logic.

Trauma silences the truth, and survival sometimes means staying quiet until you know it's safe to scream.

After the charges, I tried to go back to normal life, I tried to show up for work, be a good mom, Smile at the grocery store, but my nervous system was wrecked.

I'd flinch when someone touched my shoulder.

I'd panic if I saw a car like his friends in the parking lot, I'd hear phantom rings in my sleep, convinced he was calling again.

I was out of the "entanglement".

But the "entanglement" wasn't out of me.

Then came court day.

I sat across from him in the courtroom and didn't recognize the person I once let crawl into my bed.

He looked cold.

Arrogant.

Unbothered.

He didn't apologize.

He didn't look sorry.

He didn't even look scared.

And as I testified—voice shaking, body trembling, tears threatening—I realized this wasn't just about what he did to me. This was about reclaiming my fucking power. This was about showing my daughter what strength looks like when it's bruised and bleeding but still standing.

He was sentenced to one year.

One. Year.

For turning my life into a prison cell made of fear, threats, and trauma.

A fucking year.

But here's the thing:

I served a longer sentence than he ever did.

He got 365 days, I got a lifetime of therapy, triggers, PTSD, and learning to feel safe in my own skin again.

I tried to drop the charges, not because I forgave him, but because I wanted peace, I wanted it all to go away, to stop reliving it, to stop being the girl who "had a stalker.", To stop feeling like my body was branded with a story I didn't choose.

But the Crown said no.

Because of how severe the case was, they continued prosecution without my consent.

And honestly?

I'm glad they did.

Because back then—I didn't know I was worth protecting.

Let's talk about the shame, The shame of wanting him— even after all the things he did, yes, I still wanted him sometimes, or maybe I just wanted the version of myself I felt like when he touched me.

The confident one.

The wild one.

The untouchable sex goddess who didn't give a fuck.

But that version of me was an illusion, A trauma response in stilettos.

And I had to grieve her, too.

Healing wasn't pretty.

It didn't come with a therapist couch and a box of tissues, It looked like panic attacks in my car, It looked like double-checking every lock before bed, it looked like trying to date again and flinching when someone reached across the table too fast.

But it also looked like taking my power back.

It looked like writing this chapter.

It looked like saying his name out loud to the universe and refusing to carry the secret anymore.

Here's what I want every woman to know:

You are not weak because you stayed, you are not broken because you still miss the feeling, you are not to blame for someone else's inability to love you safely.

You were conditioned to believe that love hurts, that you should fight for it, that intensity means passion and jealousy means love.

It fucking doesn't.

Love doesn't stalk you.

Love doesn't threaten you.

Love doesn't make you feel small, scared, or silent.

That's control.

That's obsession.

That's abuse.

And you don't owe anyone an explanation for leaving, you don't have to make it make sense to anyone else.

You just have to save yourself.

And if you already did—I'm so fucking proud of you.

I didn't write this chapter to scare you.

I wrote it to say:

You're not alone.

You're not crazy.

And it's not your fault.

Not then.

Not ever.

And if no one's told you today?

I see you.

I believe you.

And I will never let you forget how fucking brave you are for surviving what no one else saw.

You are Worthy As Fuck. *

CHAPTER 7: Gaslight, Girlboss, Grieve, Repeat

"I thought I was healing. Turns out I was just trauma-decorating with inspirational quotes"

Part 1: The Narcissist I Almost Defended

Let's start with a familiar phrase:
"I wish I had a chance with a girl like you."
Sounds harmless, right? Flattering, even. The kind of thing that makes your inner teenager do a cartwheel and think, "Omg, is this my rom-com moment?"

Spoiler alert: It's not.

It's a manipulation wrapped in charm. A Trojan horse wearing cologne. And I fucking fell for it.

Now, I didn't know it was manipulation when I first read that message. I just knew that when his words lit up my inbox out of nowhere, they hit me in a place I hadn't felt in a while—my ego. My femininity. My need to feel seen. It wasn't even about him. It was about being noticed.
That's the trap.
And this guy? He knew exactly what he was doing. We weren't even Facebook friends. I had seen him around, said the occasional polite hello, but nothing that screamed "start a love story." Still, there it was— *"You're so pretty. I wish I had a chance with someone like you."*
And just like that, I smiled. I'm not proud of it, but I'm not going to lie. I was feeling myself for a hot second. Like I had just walked into a scene from Clueless, twirled my hair, and said, "As if." But then I remembered—he had a girlfriend, So I left it on read.
The Setup

A few months passed. Life moved on. I went out with friends one night, ended up at a local strip bar (don't ask,

we were chasing vibes not dicks), and who walks past my table?
Yup. Him.
He smiled. I smiled. And that same little flicker of validation came back, Later, he bought me a drink. Told me to give him my number before I left. I didn't. I wasn't stupid... yet, then he messaged me again. Same line.
"You're so beautiful. I wish I had a chance."
And this time? I took the bait.
Why? Because now he told me he was single. Apparently, his girlfriend cheated. He was just finishing renovations at her house out of the kindness of his golden fucking heart; And me? I ate that story like it was a warm brownie sundae. "Awww, he's such a good guy..." Bitch, no. He was an actor. I just didn't know the script yet.

The First Date (A.K.A. The Audition)

He came over to watch a movie. We'd been talking for weeks. I was nervous, but curious. He sat on one end of the couch. I sat on the other. We didn't touch. Didn't kiss. Just a polite hug when he left.
And of course, girl brain activated immediately.
Was it the lighting? Did I wear the wrong jeans? Should I have baked cookies? Was he not into me?

So I asked him straight-up—why no kiss?
His answer? "You're not like those girls. I was nervous."

And I swooned. Because at the time, that sounded respectful. Mature. Emotionally intelligent.

Now I know it was love bombing with a side of slow-play manipulation. When narcissists know they've got a smart woman, they don't come in hot. They play it cool. They build trust first.

And I was hooked.

We started dating. He told me he was falling in love. Then he told me he loved me.
And then?
He took it back
The Dagger
One night he just said it: "I shouldn't have told you I loved you, It hit me like a brick to the chest. I froze. What the fuck do you say to that? But then, days later, he spun it.
"It's just... I've never felt this way so fast before. It scared me."
And there it was.
A red flag wrapped in a poetic excuse. And I clung to it like a life raft.

The more confusing it got, the deeper I fell.

We posted pictures. Changed our Facebook status. Hung out with his friends and their wives. We looked like a real couple, living a real life, But behind the filtered photos? The mind games were brewing.

The Triangle

I introduced him to one of my friends and her husband. They lived a few houses down from him. We had weekly dinners together—laughing, drinking, playing house. Then one night, he was supposed to come to my house for dinner.
I called. He didn't answer.
Eventually, he picked up.

"I'm eating dinner at your friend's house."
I stopped stirring the spaghetti sauce. My blood boiled.
Wait... what? My friend? Alone? Her husband's not home? You're... what? I tried to brush it off. *They're just close... right? Isn't it great they all get along?*
But something in my gut wouldn't shut up. That anxious swirl in your stomach that whispers, *"Something isn't right here."*

He started boating with her and her kids—without me. Spending time at her house when I wasn't around, And I lost my fucking mind. I watched them like a hawk every time we hung out. I started to resent her. I accused him of liking her. I accused her of liking him. And he said I was crazy.
And the worst part?
I started believing him.

The "Confession"
One day she called me.
"Come over. I need to show you something."
I already knew. The second I saw her name light up my phone, I knew, she showed me her computer. A message from him.
Him: Hey you. How's your day going?
Her: Good. You?
Him: Better now that I'm talking to you.
There it was.
The same fucking line he used on me, I confronted him. His response?

"I didn't mean it like that."

...EXCUSE ME? In what universe does "better now that I'm talking to you" NOT sound like a flirty fucking come-on?
But he gaslit the hell out of me, told me I was insecure. That I was imagining things. That my friend was trying to break us up. That I should trust him.
I stayed.
I believed him.
I fought my instincts, invalidated my gut, and defended a man who couldn't even spell accountability.

That's what narcissistic abuse does—it convinces you that your reality isn't real.
You don't just fall for a narcissist.
You're recruited. Like a job interview where you didn't even know you applied—but somehow, you're now the entire HR department and emotional janitor.
They don't start off screaming or gaslighting. They start off perfect, it begins with love-bombing: compliments, connection, chemistry that feels divinely orchestrated. You think, finally—someone who sees me, He remembered your favorite drink. He quoted something you said in a random Tuesday convo two weeks ago. He told you he's never felt this kind of connection with anyone before. It's not real intimacy—it's information gathering.
They study you to mirror you. They don't fall in love with you—they become what you would fall in love with.
And once they, have you?
The slow, subtle fuckery begins.

The Identity Erosion

You don't even notice it at first, you start apologizing more than you used to. You second-guess yourself before you speak. You laugh less. Your light dims. He makes little comments that stick like burrs under your skin:

- *"You sure you want to wear that?"*
- *"God, you're so sensitive."*
- *"Wow, I didn't think you'd react that way."*

You start asking for permission instead of just being who you are, your world gets smaller.
Your friends annoy him. Your family stresses him out. Your hobbies aren't worth the time. Suddenly, it's just the two of you—and when it's good, it's amazing. But when it's bad? It's your fault.
And you believe it, because by now, you've been conditioned to think you're the problem.

The Rage Cycle

Here's the kicker: narcissists don't just love chaos—they need it.
But they don't start it outright. They poke the bear until you explode.
They withhold affection. They ignore your boundaries. They flirt with your friends, then call you insecure. And when you finally break down and say,
"What the fuck is going on?"
—*they say:*
"Wow, you're so dramatic."
They stay calm while you're losing it. That's the power play.
And then they say:

- *"You need help."*
- *"This is why no one stays with you."*

- *"I can't talk to you when you're like this."*

Congratulations. You've just been emotionally mugged and blamed for it.

They turn your reaction into the crime and their manipulation into the alibi, You think you're fighting to fix the relationship, but really—you're just fighting to prove you're not crazy.

That's the gaslight.

The Isolation Game

By now, you're exhausted. You're so far removed from who you were that you start forgetting what normal feels like, you've stopped talking to friends about the relationship because you don't want to hear what they'll say, you lie for him. You make excuses. You tell people you're just going through a "rough patch," but deep down, you know it's more than that.

You're grieving.

Not just him—but you.

You miss the woman you were before you started shrinking for him. Before you twisted yourself into emotional origami trying to "be less much," "cause less drama," "talk softer."

This isn't love. This is slow-drip psychological warfare, and you keep pouring from your empty cup because once upon a time, he made you feel chosen.

Now?

You feel owned.

The Breaking Point

For me, the moment I knew it was over wasn't even a fight. It was silence.

We were sitting in the same room, and I realized: I don't recognize this version of myself. Not the way I walked on eggshells. Not the way I minimized my dreams to protect his ego. Not the way I twisted my intuition into knots to avoid being called "crazy."
I missed my voice. My fire. My fucking joy.
That's the thing with emotional abuse—it doesn't always leave bruises. It leaves echoes, it's not until you're out that you realize how much of you you lost, and even then, part of you still wants to go back. Because the most addictive drug in the world?
Potential.
You keep remembering how he could be. How he used to be, but baby, that wasn't real. That was the audition.
What you got later?
That's who he really is.

The Grief You Don't See Coming

When you finally leave, you don't feel free right away, you feel fucking broken, you question yourself. Was it really that bad? Did I exaggerate it? Was I too emotional, you forget the manipulation and remember the moments. The laughs. The cuddles. The fake peace that was just a pause between storms.
But that's what trauma bonds do.
They make you crave the very thing that destroyed you, you're not missing him—you're missing the version of you that believed in him.
That's where the grief comes in.
Not just because he's gone. But because you stayed.
But guess what?
That guilt?
That pain?

That heartbreak?
That's not weakness. That's your soul waking up.
You are not stupid, you were targeted.
And now?
You're becoming the version of you who will never fall for it again.

I am worthy as fuck

Chapter 8: It's Not Mothering, It's a Fucking Boundary!

"If your love needs me to shrink, apologize, or walk in eggshells, - baby, that's not love, that's manipulation"

Let's just rip the band-aid off: when a grown-ass man looks you in the face and says, "You're not my mother," what he's really saying is: "I don't like being held accountable."
And baby, let me be the first to say—
THANK FUCKING GOD I'm not your mother.
Because if I were? You'd be grounded. Your phone would be gone. And you'd be cleaning the damn baseboards until your attitude matched your age.

But I digress.

This is the chapter I wish I didn't have to write. Because this is where the narcissistic cycle really starts to spiral. Not just gaslighting. Not just bread-crumbing. But blame-shifting with a cherry on top—where every time I asked a question, I was accused of being controlling. Overbearing. Clingy. Or the favourite insult of emotionally unavailable men everywhere: crazy.

Let me give you some backstory.

This was still the same guy from Chapter 7. Same smile. Same lies. Same manipulation dressed up as charm. I was knee-deep in the "maybe he'll change" era. You know the one. Where every red flag looks pink if you squint hard enough and believe in potential like it's a damn religion.

But this wasn't about love anymore. This was about control—his, not mine. And every time I tried to set a boundary, communicate a need, or God forbid—ask when he'd be home—I got met with some version of:
"You're not my mom."
"Stop acting like I need permission to live my life."

"Why are you always starting shit?"
Let's rewind to one of the many nights this played out.
He was going out with the boys. I was cool with that—I'm not your warden. I'm not gluing your ass to the couch. But the moment I sent a simple text at 11:43 PM:
Me: *"Hey babe, how's your night?"*
Him: *[silence]*
Midnight passed. One. Two. Bars were closed. Still nothing... there isn't anything open past 2 am other than 7-11 and legs and they sure as fuck we're not mine. Meanwhile, I'm lying in bed staring at the ceiling like a forensic detective. My stomach was in knots. And not because I was insecure. But because every goddamn time this happened, it followed the same pattern: silence → excuses → defensiveness → blame, And when he finally stumbled through the door around 3:30 AM?
"I didn't answer because I didn't want to deal with your shit."
"You always ruin my night."
"You're just insecure. That's your problem."

Oh really?

Because I'm pretty fucking secure in the fact that you're a grown man with a working phone and 14-bathroom breaks. You had time to text. You just chose not to. And instead of being honest or considerate, you flipped it around and made it my fault.

Classic narcissistic move: evade responsibility and reframe it as someone else's emotional overreaction.

I remember sitting on the edge of the bed crying while he peeled off his jacket like he was the one who had a hard night. And all I wanted—all I wanted—was for him to look at me and say, "Sorry. I should've checked in."

But no.

Instead, I got hit with, *"You should've trusted me."*

No, motherfucker. You should've respected me.

This is what so many women experience and yet rarely talk about. Because the moment we speak up, we're told we're nagging. That we're too much. That we're trying to control someone's freedom. And heaven forbid we bring up the fact that if the roles were reversed? They'd be flipping couches over a delayed response.

Let's be clear: asking for communication is not mothering. Asking for honesty is not control. Setting a boundary is not being crazy.
It's called being a fucking adult in a relationship.
And yet, every time I tried to express myself, I got punished. With silence. With sarcasm. With that same line that cut like a blade every time:

"You're not my mom."

And still, I stayed.

Because I thought if I could just phrase it differently—if I could just explain it better—he'd finally get it. That we're not in high school. That this isn't a situationship. That if you want to be treated like a grown man, act like one.

Spoiler: he never got it.

Not because he couldn't—but because he didn't want to.

He needed me to be the "crazy" one. He needed me to overreact, to spiral, to cry—so he could point the finger and say, "See? This is why I don't answer. This is why I lie. This is why I stay out all night."
He turned my reaction into justification for his disrespect.
And that's what narcissistic abuse does.
It trains you to doubt yourself. To suppress your voice. To second-guess your gut. It teaches you that you are the problem—and if you could just be less, maybe you'd be enough.

Let me say this loud and clear:

You are not too much. He is just not enough.
And if he confuses basic communication with "being controlled," that's not your man. That's a boy wearing a grown-up costume, terrified of accountability. I didn't need to be anyone's mother. I just needed to be met with mutual respect, but in his world, respect was a currency he only spent when he wanted something. And boundaries? Boundaries were treated like ultimatums.

This chapter could've ended there....

But it didn't.

Because that night—the one where I sat crying in the dark while he snored beside me like nothing happened? That was the night I made a promise, I was done being the one who always "started shit.", I was done being the one who kept her mouth shut to keep the peace, And I was done letting silence be the answer I never deserved.

It's Not Mothering, it's a Fucking Boundary: Stop Confusing Accountability with Control

The thing about boundaries is… they only piss off the people who benefitted from you having none. Once I started enforcing mine—oh, the audacity I apparently had. I wasn't yelling. I wasn't accusing. I was simply doing something radical: asking for respect. And his reaction?

Total meltdown.

He made me feel like I was out here writing curfews in Sharpie on his forehead. Like texting me back was the equivalent of house arrest. It was so over-the-top ridiculous that at one point, I actually started laughing.

"Why are you so defensive over something a literal toddler could do with one button and a thumb?"

That did not go over well.

Because men like this don't want equality in relationships—they want power. Silent power. The kind where they come and go as they please and you're just supposed to be grateful they chose you.

Well, fuck that.

Let's talk about the gaslighting greatest hits I heard on repeat every time I tried to speak my truth:

- *"If you weren't so insecure, I wouldn't act this way."*
- *"You're imagining things."*

- *"You're too emotional. It's not that serious."*
- *"You overthink everything."*
- *"You're trying to control me."*

And my all-time favourite:

"This is why I can't be myself around you."

No. You just don't want to be held accountable for who you really are.

I started noticing more of the bullshit. How he wouldn't post me online unless I begged. How he always made me feel like I was "lucky" to be with him—even though I was the one cleaning up his messes, calming his moods, making excuses to my friends, and silencing my own intuition.

That's the thing about these "not your mom" types—they want all the benefits of a supportive, nurturing woman... without actually being worthy of one.

They'll let you cook, clean, run their errands, manage their emotions, soothe their insecurities—but the second you ask for basic respect? You're overbearing. Too much. Just like their "crazy" ex.

And that's not mothering. That's emotional labor. *Unpaid.*
Unappreciated.
Unreciprocated.

Let's be honest—if your partner acts like a child, they're going to need parenting energy. But that doesn't mean we should give it. That means we should leave. The moment you start parenting your partner, you're no longer in a relationship. You're in a dynamic where love is weaponized and communication is punishment.

That's exactly what happened to me.

I stopped asking when he'd be home.
I stopped texting first.
I stopped checking in.
And guess what happened?
He accused me of not caring.

Make it make sense.

When I asked for communication, I was too needy. When I gave space, I didn't love him enough. No matter what I did—it was never right. And that's because it was never about what I was doing. It was about control.

He wanted to be in charge of how much I loved him, how I proved it, and how little he had to give in return.

And I played into it. I danced the damn dance. I apologized when I had nothing to apologize for. I tried harder when I should've walked away. I lost sleep, lost self-respect, and almost lost myself in the process.

But I didn't.

Because the truth eventually screamed louder than the excuses.

And here it is:

Respect isn't a fucking chore. It's the bare minimum.

And if a man treats you like you're being a mother for expecting it? Then let him go find someone who's okay being his babysitter. (Good luck with that, by the way.)

Because I am not here to raise anyone but my kid.
I am not your mom.
I am not your therapist.
I am not your warden.
I am not your punching bag.
I am not your emotional pacifier.
I am not the woman who will shrink herself just so you don't feel small.
I am a goddamn grown woman with needs, standards, and boundaries, and if you can't handle that? Then you were never man enough to stand beside me in the first place.

Coaching Insight & Worthy AF Wake-Up Call

Let's break this down for the badass woman reading this who's still justifying someone else's shitty behaviour.

If someone makes you feel like setting boundaries is "mothering," here's what you need to know:

- *Healthy communication ≠ control.*
  Asking where someone is, how they're doing, or when they'll be home isn't control. It's respect.
- *Your nervous system isn't dramatic. It's wise.*
  That pit in your stomach? That racing heart? That spiral of anxiety when he goes MIA. That's not you being needy. That's your body alerting you to a pattern of emotional neglect.

- *Manipulation thrives on inconsistency.*
  These men keep you in limbo on purpose. One moment they're sweet. The next, they're cold. That rollercoaster is designed to keep you chasing their approval—and questioning your reality.
- *You're allowed to want consistency.*
  That's not crazy. That's mature. That's what emotionally healthy adults do.
- *You don't have to prove you're not controlling.*
  You're not. You're communicating. And anyone who twists that into control is avoiding accountability.

Real Talk Recap

This chapter isn't just about one guy. It's about every guy who ever tried to turn your confidence into a character flaw. Whoever turned your emotions into a punchline. Who ever tried to convince you that asking for basic human decency made you too much.

Spoiler alert: you are not too much. They were just never enough.

And I'm not here to teach grown men how to be grown. I'm here to teach women how to remember who the fuck they are.

So to the woman reading this who's been made to feel crazy, needy, or "too emotional" for simply wanting clarity, communication, and commitment?

Let me remind you:

You're not crazy. You're worthy as fuck.
And he knew it.

That's why he tried to convince you otherwise.

But not anymore.

Affirmation :
I will never again let someone confuse disrespect with independence. I am not controlling—I am clear. I am not crazy—I am conscious. I am not too much—I am just enough for the right one.

I AM WORTHY AS FUCK

Chapter 9: Addicted To The Apology that Never Came

"You can't heal where you're still begging to be seen"

Let's get one thing straight right out the gate: Narcissistic abuse doesn't always come wrapped in rage and fists.
Sometimes, it comes wrapped in compliments, promises, "check-ins," and good morning texts that feel like dopamine hits. It doesn't always start with chaos, It starts with charm, that's what makes it so fucking dangerous; Because when your trauma-bonded, you don't see manipulation. You see butterflies. You don't recognize red flags. You call them quirks. And you don't call it abuse—because you're too busy blaming yourself.

Let's go back to the beginning.

The Trap Starts with "I Wish I Had a Chance"

In Chapter 7, we cracked open the door on one of the most manipulative relationships I've ever been in. He didn't walk through that door like a monster. He slithered in like a fantasy, It started with a DM.
"You're so beautiful. I wish I had a chance with someone like you.". That line should've been background noise. But instead, it hit something soft. Something wounded. Something lonely. Because narcissists are experts at spotting women who are exhausted, under-appreciated, and secretly wondering if they're still wanted.
He knew exactly how to find that part of me—and how to feed it just enough to hook me, He didn't come in screaming or love-bombing right away. He came in slow, like a snake in the grass. Just enough eye contact. Just enough interest. Just enough of a "good guy" act to make me second-guess my gut.
Narcissistic abuse doesn't start like a horror story.

It starts like a fucking rom-com.

Love-Bombing Isn't Love. It's Bait.

In the early stages, it felt like the most "normal" relationship I'd had in years. We went on dates. We watched movies. We were cute, He didn't try to sleep with me on the first night. He said he respected me. He said I wasn't "like the other girls."
(That line is always a red flag in disguise. If he disrespects other women to compliment you, RUN.)
He told me he'd never fallen so fast before. He introduced me to his friends. We did dinner with couples. Took selfies. Changed our Facebook status.
It felt safe. Too safe.
Because that's how the cycle works:
1. *Idealize*
2. *Devalue*
3. *Discard*

And if you're really "lucky"?
They'll repeat that cycle over and over until you've questioned your entire fucking reality.

Example #1: The "Oops, I Take It Back" ILY
When he told me he loved me, I melted. My walls came crashing down, finally—a man who wasn't afraid of feelings.
But a few days later?
He took it back.
Just… revoked it like a coupon that expired. He said he shouldn't have said it. That he wasn't sure. That it was too fast, and just like that—I went from loved to confused to emotionally starving. That's the point, they give you a taste of affection and then yank it away—so you'll spend the rest

of the relationship trying to earn back what they chose to give you in the first place.
That's not love. That's control.

Gaslighting: The Real Mind-fuck

Things escalated when I found out he was hanging out with my friend behind my back. Boat rides. Dinners. Time with her kids. And I wasn't invited.

Let's pause here:

If your man is spending one-on-one time with your friend while you're home making dinner
—THAT IS NOT NORMAL.
But when I brought it up, He flipped the script.
He said:

- *"You're crazy."*
- *"You're insecure."*
- *"She's like a sister to me."*

Then, when I discovered he had DM'd her with a flirty message, he said:

- *"I didn't mean it like that."*
- *"You're making it bigger than it is."*
- *"You just don't trust me."*

And you know what's fucked?
I believed him.
Because that's what gaslighting does, It turns you against yourself.

The Narcissist's Toolkit: A Quick Breakdown

Here are the top tactics narcissists use—and how they showed up in my story:

1. Love Bombing
"You're not like the others."
"I've never felt this way before."
"You're perfect."
Translation: Let me inflate your ego so you won't notice me testing your boundaries.

2. Gaslighting
"That's not what I said."
"You're crazy."
"You're too emotional."
Translation: Let me make you doubt your own memory, feelings, and instincts so I stay in control.

3. Triangulation
Flirting with your friend.
Bringing up exes.
Comparing you to other women.
Translation: Let me create competition so you feel insecure and try harder.

4. Blame Shifting
"You made me do it."
"You're always picking fights."
"You're too sensitive."
Translation: Let me avoid accountability by making you feel like the abuser.

5. Breadcrumbing
Little messages.
Small gestures.
Just enough to keep you hooked.
Translation: Let me starve you emotionally and then feed you crumbs so you don't leave.

Why We Stay: The Trauma Bond

The most common question people ask is:

"Why didn't you leave?"

Here's the truth:

Because I thought it was love, Because I believed it was my fault, because every time I tried to walk away, he'd do something kind. Say something sweet. Give just enough to confuse me.

That's a trauma bond.

It's what happens when abuse is mixed with affection, it keeps you craving the high while ignoring the crash, it's like being addicted to a drug that's destroying you—but still chasing the next hit.

Example #2: The Disrespect Dressed as "Independence"

He'd disappear during guys 'nights out. I'd text and get nothing.

Not "Hey babe, all good."

Not "Having fun, see you soon."

Nothing.

And when I asked him about it?

He said:

"What are you, my mother?"

"Stop being so controlling."

Let me say this loud for the girls in the back:

Wanting a basic level of communication is not controlling. If your partner turns your reasonable request for respect into a fight—he's not respecting your boundaries. He's trying to erase them.

Narcissistic Abuse Is Death by a Thousand Paper Cuts

It's not just the big moments; It's the everyday erosion of your identity.
- *The silent treatment after you ask for honesty*
- *The way your opinions suddenly feel "dramatic"*
- *The constant apologizing you do just to keep the peace*
- *The way you stop trusting yourself—because they never fucking validate your reality*

It's subtle. It's slippery. And it's devastating, you stop recognizing yourself, you go from confident to confused, From powerful to paranoid, From joyful to jealous.
You question every damn thing. Even your worth.
That's how they win.

Breaking the Cycle: Step One Is SEEING IT
Before you can break free, you have to see it for what it is.
Not:
- **"He's just going through a lot"**
- **"He's had a rough childhood"**
- **"He doesn't mean to hurt me"**

But:
"He is showing me who he is—and I believe him."
Every manipulation. Every lie. Every blame game.
Believe it, call it what it is, and then begin the slow, painful, empowering process of detachment.

The Breaking Point: When Fantasy Finally Cracks
There's always a moment. A crack. A shift in your gut that won't shut up anymore.
For me, it wasn't some big blow-up or discovery.
It was something smaller, it was realizing I had stopped laughing, not because I didn't want to—but because I didn't even recognize joy in myself anymore. I was tired all the time. Hyper-vigilant. Like I had to earn my own relationship, every fucking day.

One night, he came home at 4 a.m. again. Same excuses. Same sigh. Same dismissive, "I don't wanna talk about this."
I was crying in the bathroom with a towel shoved in my mouth so I wouldn't wake up my kid.
And it hit me:
I am literally hiding my pain like a crime.
That was my breaking point.
Not the cheating. Not the gaslighting.
But the moment I saw myself and didn't recognize the woman in the mirror.
That girl? That version of me?
She was dying inside a relationship I kept calling "love."

The Withdrawal Is Real—and Brutal

Leaving a narcissist isn't just a breakup. It's a detox.

You go through literal withdrawal symptoms:
- *Anxiety*
- *Panic attacks*
- *Sleepless nights*
- *Cravings to reach out*
- *Guilt*
- *Shame*
- *Self-doubt*
- *Obsessively replaying conversations in your head trying to "make it make sense"*

And if you're not careful, you'll go back just to make the pain stop.
That's why trauma bonds are so fucking hard to break, you think you're missing him, but you're actually just missing the highs he used to give you between the chaos.

What Helped Me Let Go

I didn't wake up one day magically healed. I had to unlearn every single lie that man—and my own trauma—had taught me about love.

Here's what actually helped:

1. Naming It

Saying the words out loud:

"This was narcissistic abuse."

"This was gaslighting."

"This was not my fault."

When you name the pattern, you take away its power.

2. Writing Letters I Never Sent

I wrote letters to him. Not to send—but to purge.

I said everything I couldn't say out loud. I gave my pain a voice. I gave my grief a grave.

Sometimes I cursed him out, Sometimes I cried. Sometimes I mourned the version of me who stayed.

It was messy. But it was necessary.

3. Blocking Without Guilt

Blocking isn't petty. It's protection, You don't owe someone who broke you a front-row seat to your healing. I didn't need to prove I was over him. I needed to get free of the fucking hook he still had in my nervous system. So, I blocked his number. Blocked his socials. Removed mutual friends.

And when I got tempted to look him up?

I reminded myself that healing means not feeding the wound.

4. Affirmation + Action = Rewiring

I didn't just say "I am worthy., I started acting like it.

I made a list of all the shit I had accepted that I never would again, I created new rules—ones that protected my peace, not my relationship status.

And I reminded myself:

"The version of you that begged to be chosen is gone. The version of you that chooses herself.

She's just getting started."

The Red Flag Decoder (aka Trusting Your Gut Again)

One of the hardest parts of recovery is learning to trust yourself again, you start second-guessing everything. Was it really abuse? Did I overreact? Am I just too sensitive?
NO.
You're not too sensitive. You're not crazy. And you didn't imagine the manipulation.

Here's a list I made in my journal—and I want you to copy it, screenshot it, tattoo it on your heart if you have to:
If it feels like a red flag… it probably is.
Let me break down some of the most common ones:

"You're just too emotional."

Translation: I don't want to deal with your reaction to my disrespect.

"I didn't lie—I just didn't tell you."

Translation: I withhold truth to maintain power.

"You're overthinking it."

Translation: You're getting close to the truth, and I don't like it.

"Why are you always starting fights?"

Translation: You're holding me accountable, and that's inconvenient.

Silent treatment

This is emotional abuse dressed up as "needing space."

"You'll never find anyone better than me."

Oh honey—don't make me laugh.

The only thing I'd never find again is someone who made me feel that small and called it love.

Rewiring Your Nervous System After Narcissistic Abuse

Let's get into some science.

Narcissistic abuse isn't just emotional—it's physiological.

Your nervous system gets stuck in fight-or-flight.

Your brain becomes hyper-alert to tone, silence, pauses in texting, you lose your baseline of safety.

And when you leave?

Your body is still reacting to triggers that aren't even there anymore.

Here's what helped me heal somatically:

1. Daily Nervous System Check-Ins

Ask yourself:
- *Am I grounded?*
- *Am I breathing shallow?*
- *Is this emotion mine—or is it a trauma response?*

I'd pause and do breath-work or shake out my limbs. Literally discharging that nervous energy from my body.

2. Journal Prompts
- *What version of me tolerated this?*
- *What did I believe about love that kept me stuck?*
- *What do I need to feel safe again?*

3. EFT Tapping

I'd tap while saying things like:
- *"Even though I felt like I wasn't enough, I deeply and completely love and accept myself."*
- *"Even though I stayed too long, I forgive myself."*

It rewired my self-blame into self-compassion.

4. Somatic Releasing

I'd do movement.
Baths.
Stretching.
Screaming into pillows.
Crying without trying to stop.

I let my body say what my mouth couldn't.

The Mirror Moment: Who You Become After Narcissistic Abuse

I didn't just walk away from that relationship. I walked back to myself, To the woman who forgot how powerful she is, To the version of me that had needs, boundaries, and desires, To the girl who thought love meant sacrificing everything just to be seen.

Narcissistic abuse doesn't just teach you who someone else is, it teaches you who you are when you're finally done pretending, you're okay, It teaches you that you're not needy. You're not dramatic. You're not crazy.

You're someone who was trained to tolerate crumbs—and now you're hungry for the whole fucking table.

The Pattern: I Thought It Was Love (But It Was Just Control in Disguise)

When Abuse Doesn't Look Like Abuse

Let's talk about the quiet kind of narcissistic abuse, The kind that doesn't leave bruises, The kind that makes you question yourself more than your partner, The kind that masquerades as romance.

It sounds like:
- *"I just want to be with you all the time."* (Isolation)
- *"No one else understands me like you do."* (Guilt-tripping)
- *"I hate when you go out without me."* (Control masked as affection)

- *"Why are you wearing that? You're mine."* (Jealousy disguised as love)
- *"You're so lucky I put up with you."* (Nagging)

These are not compliments.
They're subtle manipulations.
And they chip away at your self-worth one cracked compliment at a time.
fucking reality.

Stop Trying to Fix What Was Never Yours to Heal

Let me be blunt:

You are not the rehabilitation centre for emotionally unavailable men.

You are not the emotional sponge for a grown-ass man who refuses to get therapy.

You are not his mother, his savior, or his emotional support animal.

You're a woman. A whole woman.

And your job is not to heal someone who keeps cutting you just to see if you'll bleed love. You don't fix a narcissist. You walk away before they rewrite your entire identity.

Real Boundaries for the Post-Abuse Era

So what does Worthy AF love look like after narcissistic abuse? It looks like boundaries, Unapologetic, non-negotiable, peace-protecting boundaries, and if you're wondering where to start, here's a cheat sheet:

Boundary #1:
If you ghost me, I block you.
Not out of pettiness. Out of protection.

Boundary #2:
If you raise your voice to win, I walk.
We don't weaponize tone in this house.

Boundary #3:
If you flirt to get validation, I leave.
I'm not competing with your self-worth issues.

Boundary #4:
If you call me crazy, we're done.
That word is abuse in a cute little costume.
Boundary #5:
If you can't communicate like a grown adult, I'm not parenting you through conversations.
This ain't pre-K.
Boundary #6:
If my nervous system feels unsafe, I'm out.
That's not butterflies. That's your trauma radar screaming RUN.

These aren't walls.
They're gates—and only those who respect the key get access.

What I Wish I Could Say to Her (Letter to My Past Self)
To the girl who thought she had to stay:
To the woman who cried into her pillow, who turned off her phone just to avoid reading one more lie, To the version of me who stayed silent just to keep the peace...
This is for you.

Dear Me,
I'm so fucking proud of you.
You don't even know it yet, but you're already healing. Every tear you cried alone wasn't weakness—it was you washing off the lies. You thought it was love because he made you feel seen.

But baby, he only saw the parts of you he could control.

You're not crazy.

You're not dramatic.

You're not hard to love.

You were just starved for the kind of connection that doesn't come with conditions.

And now?

Now, you get to rebuild.

Not from scraps—but from truth.

Your truth.

You get to fall in love again—with yourself first.

You get to laugh without guilt.

You get to trust without needing to explain why you need a damn text back.

You get to be free.

And most of all?

You get to walk away from anything that makes you feel like you're too much and not enough at the same fucking time.

I love you.

I forgive you.

I honour you.

And we're never going back.

—Future You

Final Word: This Is Where the Cycle Ends

Narcissistic abuse doesn't end when the relationship ends, it ends when you reclaim your reality, It ends when you stop gaslighting yourself, It ends when you stop making excuses for red flags and start building a new life out of your goddamn non-negotiables.

It ends here.

You survived what was meant to silence you.

Now?
You become the version of you who refuses to let silence win.

Affirmation to Close the Chapter:

I am worthy as fuck.
Not because someone said I was.
Not because I was chosen.
But because I finally chose myself.

Because

I am Worthy AF

Chapter 10: The Aftermath: I Am Not Enough

"When you don't trust yourself, you'll chase people that don't deserve you"

When You Hand Over Your Power Without Realizing It

Put the damn book down for a second. Close your eyes. Say this out loud:

"I am not enough."

Feel that shit in your bones? That ache in your chest? That pit in your stomach, That's the poison talking and let me be real clear: it's not your truth.

But it feels like it is—because you've been carrying it around for so long, it's settled into your cells like trauma dust.

Every woman—every fucking woman —has whispered those four words to herself in the dark. Maybe after a fight, maybe after sex that felt more like a transaction than a connection, maybe while scrolling social media, comparing herself to the perfectly filtered illusion of "happy."

Or maybe after he left. Or cheated. Or ghosted. Or stayed but treated her like she was disposable.

Let me tell you something that'll slap the shame right out of you:

We say 'I am not enough 'when we've given everything to someone who gave us breadcrumbs and told us it was a damn buffet.

We Hand Over Our Power Dressed as Love

This chapter isn't about him.

It's about what happens after.
After you stayed too long.
After you made excuses for his behaviour.
After you contorted yourself to be more accommodating, more nurturing, more fun, more sexy, more quiet, more... whatever the hell you thought might finally make him love you the way you loved him.

Let's break it down:

You gave him your mind, your body, your emotional labor, your time, your dreams, your strength—hell, sometimes

your money, too. You thought that if you loved him hard enough, deep enough, patiently enough, it would heal him. That he would finally see you, finally pick you, finally choose you fully and forever.
But what happened?
You ended up choosing him so many times that you forgot to choose yourself, you turned your power into a goddamn sacrifice. And then you bled for a man who wouldn't even give you a Band-Aid and when it all imploded—when the truth you'd been avoiding couldn't be ignored anymore—you sat there, numb and hollow, whispering:
"I am not enough."

The Inherited Disease of Self-Abandonment

We didn't pull that phrase out of nowhere, by the way. It's inherited, Passed down.
Generation after generation of women taught to pour and pour and pour… until their own cups were bone dry, taught that love means self-sacrifice.
That a "good woman" is patient. Supportive. Silent.
Ever notice how men are raised to be kings, while women are raised to be the castle?
Support him. Shelter him. Feed him. Protect him. Sacrifice for him.
And God forbid you put yourself first—because then you're selfish, cold, difficult. A bitch.

Nah, sis. Fuck that.

We're not castles anymore.
We're the fucking storm that takes the whole system down.
But to do that—we have to stop confusing love with losing ourselves.

Rebuilding After the Breakdown: Trust, Truth, and the Voice That Lies

Let's talk about that voice.
You know the one.
The one that shows up when you're vulnerable, alone, or scrolling at 11:43 PM wondering why everyone else looks so damn happy.
It's that smug little bitch whispering:
- *"You should've seen the red flags."*
- *"You stayed too long—again."*
- *"You let him treat you like that."*
- *"No one's ever going to love you the way you want."*

She sounds like you, doesn't she?
But that voice?
She's not truth.
She's trauma with a megaphone.
And the reason she's so loud is because, for too long, you trusted him more than you trusted yourself.

The Day You Stopped Trusting Yourself
There's a moment—we all have one—when you realize you betrayed your own intuition, you ignored the pit in your stomach, you quieted your gut when it told you he wasn't it, you soothed yourself with "he's just tired" or "he didn't mean it" or "it's not that bad"
while the real you—the raw, radiant, worthy-as-fuck you—was screaming inside to get out and when it all came crashing down, you didn't just mourn the relationship You mourned your ability to trust yourself. Because how the hell could someone so smart, so strong, so intuitive...be so damn wrong?

Here's the truth that will punch you in the chest and then kiss your forehead:

You weren't wrong for loving him, you were wrong for abandoning yourself in the process.
Loving someone doesn't make you stupid.
It makes you human.
It makes you hope.
It makes you brave as hell.
But when love becomes self-erasure? When you become so focused on proving your worth to someone who can't see it, that's not love anymore, That's performance.

And baby, this is the chapter where the performance ends.

Let's Get Practical: The Trust Rebuild
Rebuilding trust in yourself isn't about perfection.
It's about reconnection.
Try this:
Every morning, before the noise of the world floods in, ask yourself two questions:
1. *What do I need today?*
2. *What boundary am I not honouring?*

Then write the answers. No editing. No sugar-coating.
Just truth.
This isn't about fixing your flaws.
It's about finding your voice underneath all the bullshit.
Because here's what happens when you stop listening to your intuition for too long:
- *You start asking everyone else for advice about your own damn life.*
- *You second-guess your decisions, even the small ones.*
- *You outsource your power.*
- *You shrink. You doubt. You disappear.*

Let me be loud for the ones in the back:

You don't need a man to validate your worth. You need to validate your own damn self.

Your intuition isn't broken.

It's just been gaslit, ignored, and buried under years of being told to "calm down," "stop being dramatic," or "be more understanding."

But she's still in there.

And when you start listening again. Your entire life shifts.

Throwing Out the Lemon: Your Comeback Starts Now

There's a reason I said throw the lemon out Because let's be honest—how many of us were taught to take shit situations and "sweeten them up"?

Add sugar.
Dilute it.
Tell ourselves it's not that bad.
Lie.

I love a good Margarita but not when its poured lies disguised as ice.

We stayed in the name of loyalty, we gave benefit after benefit of the doubt, We drank the damn Margarita and called it healing.

But healing isn't soft or sweet.

Healing is raw. Loud. Messy as hell.

It's ugly crying in the mirror because you don't recognize your reflection anymore.

It's deleting the text before you send it.

It's blocking the number you used to pray would light up your phone.

Healing is throwing the fucking lemon out and refusing to justify the taste anymore.

Because here's what they don't tell you:

You can't fully reclaim your self-worth while still nursing someone else's ego.

You can't pour from an empty cup—and girl, you've been scraping the sides for years.

The Breaking Point: When You Finally Choose You
You know that moment.
Not the first time he lied. Not the second time he disappeared for hours. Not even the time he blamed you for his cheating because you were "too emotional."
No,
the moment you truly woke up Was when you realized this:
You would rather be alone and rebuilding… than together and disappearing.

THAT was the day you stopped begging someone to treat you like you mattered.
THAT was the day your energy came home.
THAT was the day you stopped auditioning for a role in someone else's story—and picked up the pen to write your own.

The Truth About "Enough"

Let's go back to that core wound: "I am not enough."
Where the fuck did it even come from?
Maybe it started in childhood when you were told you were "too sensitive, maybe it was reinforced in high school when you weren't the girl they picked, maybe it grew legs in your 20s when you kept choosing projects instead of partners, hoping you could love them into loving you.
But no matter where it came from, here's where it ends:
Right here. Right now. With you.
You don't become enough by achieving more, shrinking smaller, being sexier, cooler, less "emotional," or more agreeable, you become enough the second you stop chasing someone else's definition of it.

You were enough the day you were born.
You were enough before your first heartbreak.
You were enough even when you broke down in a grocery store aisle with a baby on your hip and mascara running down your face.

You didn't lose your worth.
You just forgot how to see it.

Let's Talk Boundaries—For Real This Time
Here's what Worthy AF women know:

- *Boundaries aren't walls. They're standards.*
- *Saying "no" doesn't make you a bitch. It makes you a woman who knows her value.*
- *You don't owe access to anyone just because they "used to be close."*
- *You are not rude for protecting your peace.*

Let me be real:
If someone gets angry or defensive when you set a boundary, that's not a partner—it's a parasite. I used to think I had to explain or justify every boundary I set.
Now?
I say it once.
You cross it? You're done.
No second conversation. No PowerPoint slides on "Why This Boundary Matters."
If they can't respect it, they don't get a seat at your table.

The "I Am Enough" Ritual

Here's the ritual I give every client, every friend, and every fierce-ass woman rebuilding after betrayal:
Each morning:
1. *Stand in front of a mirror.*
2. *Look yourself in the eyes. Like really look. Through the pain. Through the fear. Through the old stories.*

3. *Say this out loud:*
**I am not broken.
I am not too much.
I am not hard to love.
I am not replaceable.
I am not crazy.
I am not a burden.
I am ENOUGH. Exactly as I am. Unfiltered. Unapologetic. Unfuckwithable."**
Repeat it 3 times.
Every day.
Even when you don't believe it. Especially when you don't believe it.
Because repetition rewires the brain.
Neuroplasticity is real and that voice inside you—the one that whispers doubt—she's not the truth.
She's the ghost of the girl who forgot her worth.
And she's not in charge anymore.

Stop Giving First-Place Energy to Last-Place People

You can't win your life back if you keep watering the dead plants. That man who ghosted you?
The one who made you beg for the bare minimum?
The one who said he was "just confused" or "not ready" or "you're too good for me" (aka the emotionally unavailable national anthem)?
Stop romanticizing him.
He wasn't a missed opportunity.
He was a mirror—showing you where your self-worth still needed reinforcement.

And every time you try to resurrect that past version of yourself to get him back, you're burying the Worthy AF woman you're becoming.
You don't need to "win" a man back who couldn't even keep you when you were crumbling.

Your New Definition of Enough

You are enough when:
- *You trust your gut more than a sweet-talking mouth.*
- *You speak your needs out loud without apologizing.*
- *You walk away the first time you feel unsafe.*
- *You stop chasing potential and start choosing peace.*
- *You fall in love with your solitude—and stop fearing your silence.*

Because being "enough" isn't a finish line.
It's a decision you make daily and the day you decide you're enough. Its the day your entire life starts to shift.

Final Words of Chapter 10

You don't need to be less sensitive You need to stop giving your sensitivity to people who don't deserve it, you don't need to fix your body, you need to fix your mirror, you don't need to shrink, you need to expand into your power.
The aftermath doesn't define you.
What you do next does.
So, here's what I want you to do:
Close this chapter.
Write yourself a letter—not to him, not to your past, not to your pain.
But to you.
To the version of you who's still learning to rise.
To the one who never stopped hoping.

To the one who knows, even though the tears and broken dreams, that she's worthy of more.

Write it. Read it. Frame it if you have to.
And end it with the affirmation that will carry you through every storm:

I am worthy as fuck.

Chapter 11: What The Fuck Wellness

"No amount of green juice will fix what your unhealed trauma keeps bingeing on"

The Cult of Wellness and the Lie We Bought

Let's get one thing straight before we even begin. You cannot detox your way into self-worth.
No juice cleanse.
No $79 face mask.
No macro-counting app.
No 5 a.m. hot yoga class.
None of it is going to fill the void you feel inside if you don't believe—at your core—that you are worthy of rest, nourishment, and joy.

We have been sold the biggest lie in the entire self-help and wellness industry That if you just drink more water, take the supplements, and follow the "that girl" morning routine—you'll finally feel good enough.

Here's what no one tells you:
- *You can eat kale and still hate your fucking life.*
- *You can post your gym selfies and still cry in the shower.*
- *You can do everything "right" and still feel like a fraud.*

Because the issue was never your gut health or your sleep schedule—it was your self-worth, and the billion-dollar wellness industry knows it. It's preying on your need to feel enough. And it's making a fortune doing it.

I know this because I bought into it. All of it. I Tried to Heal with Hustle There was a point in my life when I was doing everything "right" on paper.

I had the supplements lined up on the counter like soldiers, I counted every macro like it was the gospel, I wore a Fitbit, tracked my cycle, only drank out of a Stanley cup, and avoided gluten like it was Satan himself But I was still anxious. Still overwhelmed. Still emotionally spiralling when my daughter left a wet towel on the floor or someone didn't text me back.

Why?
Because none of that fixes the real wound.
I didn't trust myself.
I didn't know how to rest without guilt.
I didn't know how to eat a piece of cake without punishing myself the next day.
I didn't know how to feel beautiful unless someone else told me I was.
I had replaced emotional healing with productivity.
I thought I could bio-hack my way out of low self-worth.
Spoiler: I couldn't.

The Comparison That's Killing You
Let's talk about the fucking trap: COMPARISON.
Every time you scroll, you're subconsciously measuring your life against someone else's filtered highlight reel You know what I'm talking about.
That girl who always looks flawless at 7 a.m.
The mom who bakes the damn gluten-free muffins for school events, The influencer with the yoga body and the perfectly aesthetic kitchen. You're sitting on your bathroom floor, wondering why you feel like a failure—when you've already done three loads of laundry, made lunch for your kid, answered work emails, and fought off a full-blown panic attack.
But all you can focus on is how she looks like she has it all together.
It's not just toxic.
It's soul-destroying.
Because comparison doesn't just steal joy. It breeds shame—and shame makes you forget who the fuck you are.

When Your Health Obsession Is Just Disguised Shame

Let's get real about something no one wants to admit: A lot of what we call "wellness" is just fear in a cute Lululemon outfit.

For years, I convinced myself I was "healing" because I was buying organic chicken and avoiding dairy but behind all the health goals and Pinterest-worthy meal prep?
I was terrified.
Terrified of gaining weight.
Terrified of being seen as lazy.
Terrified of being judged for not being put together.
Terrified of being the "bad mom" who feeds her kid KD and doesn't read bedtime stories every damn night.

It wasn't wellness. It was perfectionism with probiotics and that shit will kill you slower than McDonald's, but just as painfully Because when your worth is tied to how healthy, skinny, or disciplined you are…
You will never, ever feel safe in your body.

Let's talk about the inflamed truth.
I used to think I had a hormone problem. A gut problem. A metabolism problem.
And maybe, medically, I did.
But the biggest problem?
I hated myself.
I was living in a state of fight-or-flight 24/7. My nervous system was jacked, My cortisol was through the fucking roof, I was wired but exhausted, Craving sugar but terrified to eat it, working out to "feel good" but secretly punishing my body for not being smaller.
And you want to know what the worst part was?
People praised me for it.
"Wow, you're so healthy."

"You're so disciplined."
"I wish I had your willpower."
No one knew I was crying in the closet at night; No one knew I was popping magnesium like it was candy and calling it self-care, No one knew I didn't even know what joy felt like anymore.
Because I was so busy trying to be "enough"—through wellness.

Green Juice Won't Heal the Wound of Not Feeling Good Enough

I had the mason jars, The collagen powders, The 10-step skincare routine, The protein bars that tasted like cardboard but were only 3g net carbs, so I fucking ate them anyway.
But I still looked in the mirror and saw someone I didn't recognize.

And not because of my body. Because of the emptiness I had built my identity on fixing myself on constantly trying to become "better."
But better for who?
The patriarchy? The wellness bloggers who never struggled with food, my ex who used to comment on my body but couldn't manage his own damn trauma?

Nah. Fuck that.

Healing doesn't come in a bottle, or a macros tracker Healing comes when you stop trying to earn your worth. You were never broken to begin with.

Let's Burn the Wellness Rulebook

So here's the deal.
You can absolutely love your greens and your walks and your skincare routine.
You can absolutely strive for health and still be healing but check your intention.
Ask yourself:
- *Am I doing this because I love myself… or because I'm afraid of not being enough?*
- *Am I choosing this food because it feels good in my body… or because I feel like I "should"?*
- *Am I skipping that event because I need rest… or because I feel too ashamed to show up?*

If your answer comes from fear, control, shame, or self-loathing…
It's not wellness. Its punishment dressed up as self-improvement.
And babe, you deserve better.
You deserve to live in a body that feels like home—not a battlefield, you deserve to rest without guilt, you deserve to eat the fucking cupcake without spiraling, you deserve to exist without having to earn your spot at the table.
Because you are worthy as fuck—even on your messiest, bloated, haven't-showered-in-three-days kind of day.

Your Body's Not the Problem—Your Shame Is

I don't care how much protein you eat, how low your inflammation markers are, how many steps you get in. If you still look in the mirror and hear, **"You're not enough,"**
then the real sickness isn't in your gut.
It's in your belief system.
Let me say that louder for the girl who's hiding behind the supplement drawer and calling it "health": If your self-

worth is based on your weight, your skin, your output, your appearance—
then you're not healing. You're performing and babe, this world has taught women to perform from the jump.
Be quiet.
Be pretty.
Be pleasing.
Be thin, but not too thin.
Be confident but not intimidating.
Be healthy but not obsessed.

You're not crazy for chasing worth in your body.
You were conditioned to do that but here's the most radical thing you can do in a world that profits off your shame Refuse to see yourself as a project that needs fixing.
Let's stop calling it motivation when it's actually self-rejection.
I used to call it discipline Tracking every bite. Measuring my success by my pant size but what I was actually doing? Starving for approval.
Begging my reflection to love me, begging someone else to finally say I was good enough—so I could believe it.
But healing is not a fucking aesthetic.
It's not cute or clean or marketable.
Sometimes, healing looks like gaining 10 pounds, because you finally stopped starving yourself.
Sometimes it looks like skipping the gym and sitting your ass in therapy.
Sometimes it looks like letting go of the "wellness lifestyle" that was actually a cage.
It took me years to realize that my body was never the enemy.
My shame was.

The glow-up they didn't see coming. Loving yourself without earning it.
People don't know what to do with a woman who owns her power. They especially don't know what to do when she does it with cellulite, stretch marks, and a don't-give-a-fuck attitude.

Let me tell you what healed me:
Not the green juice.
Not the 6am workouts.
Not the endless rules I tortured myself with.
It was the moment I looked in the mirror, saw my exhausted, puffy, post-crying face, and whispered:
"You're still worthy."
It was the day I stopped punishing my body and started listening to her.
The day I stopped earning rest.
The day I stopped waiting for permission to love myself.

Here's your new Worthy AF wellness manifesto:
- *Your health is not a punishment—it's a gift.*
- *Your body is not an ornament—it's a fucking miracle.*
- *You don't need to earn food, rest, love, or joy.*
- *You are allowed to heal messy.*
- *You are allowed to take up space—even when you're not at your "goal weight."*
- *You don't owe anyone perfection.*
- *You're allowed to eat the fucking cookie without journaling about it after.*

And babe—listen close—
Your worth is not found in a detox, a scale, or a fucking fitness tracker.
It's in the truth that you were worthy the whole damn time.
You just forgot.

You were distracted by the noise.
By the ads.
By the influencers who sell you shame in a pastel aesthetic.
So let this be the reminder:

You're not a before picture.
You're not unfinished.
You're not too much.
You're not broken.
You're a whole ass masterpiece—exactly as you are.

Worthy AF Affirmation to end Chapter 11:

I am worthy as fuck.
Even when I feel bloated.
Even when I skipped the gym.
Even when I ate carbs, cried in the bathroom, and didn't check a single box on my to-do list.
I am not a project.
I am a fucking revolution.

And my healing doesn't need to look pretty.
It just needs to be mine.

I am worthy AF

Chapter 12: Motherhood And Guilt: The Unpaid Internship From Hell

"No one warns you that the hardest part of motherhood is forgiving yourself daily"

Thelma, Louise, and the Guilt That Drove Me Off a Cliff (But Didn't Kill Me

Let's talk about the kind of guilt that doesn't just whisper in your ear—it screams in your face while you're trying to wipe your tears and pack a lunch at the same damn time.

I'm talking about mom guilt.

The kind that shows up not when you're fucking up—but when you're just trying to survive and let me say this loud for the women in the back who are balancing breakdowns with ballet recitals:

Mom guilt doesn't knock. It crashes. And it always rides shotgun with whatever life explosion you're trying to manage.
Divorce? Guilt.
Financial stress? Guilt.
Trying to keep your shit together while healing trauma so you don't pass it down? Guilt. On. Steroids.

It's like Thelma and fucking Louise. You and your guilt, hand in hand, flying off the edge of emotional cliffs—

except this isn't a movie. There's no cut to black. You've still gotta get up the next morning and be the soft place for your child to land. Even when your own world feels like a goddamn war zone.

But let me tell you something about that journey.
It made me.
It built the woman you see now.
And most importantly—it didn't break my daughter. It freed her.

When I say I carried guilt like luggage, I mean I dragged that shit through every season of motherhood

I felt guilty for leaving her dad.
I felt guilty for staying as long as I did.
I felt guilty for not being able to give her the "perfect" family.
I felt guilty when I worked too much, cried too much, forgot to buy the damn juice boxes, and couldn't afford the fancy vacations like the moms on Instagram.
I felt guilty for all the things she never even asked for.

Because that's what happens when you're healing your own trauma—you overcompensate. You want to give your kid everything you didn't get. You want to protect them from every wound you didn't know how to heal.

And guess what? That pressure? It'll crush you if you let it but somewhere between the sleepless nights and the self-help books, I realized something: I don't need to be a perfect mom. I need to be a healing human Because that's what she needed to see.
Let me back up and tell you the truth.
My daughter didn't grow up watching a woman who had it all together She grew up watching a woman rebuild herself, she watched me fall apart—and then fucking rise, she watched me choose peace over perfection. Boundaries over burnout. Self-worth over self-sacrifice, she saw the ugly cry breakdowns and the late-night journal sessions. The nights I said no to people-pleasing and yes to myself.
She saw the glow-up from the inside out, and because of that... she never had to guess what resilience looks like. She lived it. Every damn day.
But don't get it twisted—it wasn't all pretty. There were days I yelled when I meant to be gentle, there were nights I clung to her because I was so scared I'd already ruined her, there were moments when I gave her my smile but was too hollow inside to feel the joy myself. That's what mom guilt

does—it tells you that because you're hurting, you're failing.

But here's the truth I wish someone had tattooed on my forehead when I was in the thick of it You can be healing and still be a good mom, you can be messy and magical at the same damn time, you can cry in the bathroom and still raise a child who knows they are deeply loved.

Healing while parenting is the ultimate act of generational rebellion.

And let me tell you—I rebelled the fuck out of every toxic pattern I came from, I never wanted my daughter to inherit my wounds, So I gave her what I didn't have: honesty, I told her the truth—age appropriately, but always authentically, I didn't lie and say I was fine when I wasn't. I didn't pretend to be superwoman.
Instead, I showed her what strength actually looks like:
Apologizing when I snapped.
Owning my triggers instead of blaming her.
Letting her see me take breaks. Letting her see me say no. Letting her hear me say things like:
"Mommy's working on healing today. That means I need some quiet time. That doesn't mean I don't want to be with you. It means I want to show up better for you."
And over time? That changed her She learned boundaries. Self-respect. Emotional safety Not because I preached it—but because I practiced it.
Even when it was fucking hard.
— and yes, we're still going full throttle off that damn cliff, but this time with healing in the driver's seat.

Let's get one thing straight: Mom guilt doesn't show up because you're a bad mom It shows up because you give a damn.
You give a damn about their future.
You give a damn about breaking cycles.
You give a damn that they never feel what you felt growing up—unseen, unheard, unloved.
And sometimes, that "give a damn" will eat you alive Especially when you're doing it alone.
Single motherhood?
That shit isn't for the weak It's for the warriors who show up to parent-teacher night in tears because they just left work and haven't had time to breathe, let alone shower, It's for the moms who cry while making grilled cheese and still say "I love you" before bed, It's for the women who didn't just birth babies—they birthed new versions of themselves, over and over again, through every phase of motherhood and heartbreak and healing.

There were nights I stayed up replaying every moment of the day, Did I say the right thing, Did I hug her enough, Did she notice I was distracted when she showed me her art project?

Guilt. Guilt. Guilt.

And then I'd hear her snoring softly in her room, peaceful and safe, and I'd realize: I'm doing better than I think I am Because she's not scared of me, she trusts me, she comes to me when something hurts, she laughs freely. She cries freely. She doesn't walk on eggshells like I used to.

That didn't happen by accident. That happened because I fucking worked for it.

And if I'm being completely honest?
There were moments I thought I was breaking her, When I was overwhelmed, When I lost my temper.
When I couldn't afford the latest whatever, When I was so exhausted from surviving that I didn't have it in me to bake the damn cupcakes for the school party.

But here's what I learned—and this one's big:

Our kids don't need Pinterest-perfect. They need presence.

They need to see real.
They need to see recovery.
They need to see what it looks like when someone chooses growth even when it's gritty and hard.
My daughter didn't need me to be flawless.
She needed to see me rise, she needed to see me fall and still choose to get back up—not just for her, but for myself.
Because one day, she'll go through her own shit.
And I never wanted her to think that struggle made her broken I wanted her to know that struggle is where the strength gets forged.

I once read a quote that said, "Your greatest contribution to the world may not be something you do, but someone you raise."

And I felt that in my fucking bones.
Because this girl?
She's fierce.
She's grounded.
She's soft without apology and strong without bitterness.

And it's not because I was the perfect mom, it's because I let her see me become, I let her witness the tears, the boundaries, the glow-ups, the deep conversations, the hard decisions.
She saw the real shit—the Worthy AF woman in the making.
And even though I still have my moments—because I know this for sure:
She didn't grow up in trauma. She grew up in transformation.

And that... that's the win.

This one's for every cycle-breaking, guilt-carrying, truth-telling mama who chose healing over hiding. Let's fucking go.

You ever look at your kid and think,
"I would've given anything to be this safe as a child"?
That's when it hits you, you didn't ruin them, you rewrote the script and holy shit, that's powerful Because while you were dragging yourself through rock bottom, you were planting seeds.

Seeds of self-worth.
Seeds of emotional intelligence.
Seeds of radical, no-BS love.

I used to panic that every argument, every overwhelmed sigh, every meltdown I had in front of her was going to be what stuck.

But it wasn't.

What stuck was the way I came back.

The way I apologized.
The way I let her see me cry, then rise.

Because I wasn't just healing me.
I was showing her what healing looks like—in real-time, Breaking cycles doesn't mean they never see pain It means they don't inherit it like some messed-up family heirloom, It means they learn how to process it, It means they don't blame themselves for your bad day.

They know it's not about them Because you told them. You showed them. You loved them through it, I didn't have a manual for this, I was building the plane mid-air.
But I made a vow:
She will not need therapy because I couldn't do mine, she will not question her worth because I never claimed mine, she will not stay in toxic love just because she saw me normalize it.
And yeah... there are still moments that haunt me.
Like when I had nothing left to give but still had to smile.
Or when she asked me, "Mommy, are you sad?" and I lied.
But the truth is, I wasn't sad.
I was just fucking tired.
Tired from doing it alone.
Tired from pretending I was fine.
Tired from holding it all together with duct tape and Dunkaroos.

But here's the miracle in the mess She never needed me to be perfect, she needed me to be real and real is what saved us both.
You want to talk about guilt?
Let's talk about the guilt of...
- *Not being able to give them the life you imagined.*
- *Snapping when you're overstimulated and under-supported.*

- *Grieving the version of motherhood you thought you'd have.*

But guess what?
Guilt is the price we pay when we give a shit And I'd rather feel guilt than be the mom who feels nothing, Guilt means you care.
But it doesn't mean you're failing.

So, if you're reading this and you're knee-deep in mom guilt right now?

Let me say this loud enough for your inner critic to hear:

You are not failing.
You are fucking rising.
Even if it's messy.
Even if it's not on schedule.
Even if it doesn't look like the curated bullshit online.
You're teaching your kid something those Pinterest-perfect mamas never could. That strength isn't about smiling through it; It's about feeling it and still choosing to lead with love.
And if you ask me, that's the most Worthy AF legacy there is.

Final Truth Drop:

If mom guilt and healing had a Facebook status, it would be: It's complicated but that doesn't mean it's impossible. You're allowed to fuck up and be phenomenal, you're allowed to fall apart and raise greatness, you're allowed to be a work-in-progress and a safe space.

So take a deep breath, mama.

You're not driving off a cliff.

You're rewriting the damn road map.

And your daughter or son they are watching you blaze a trail, so they'll never have to start at rock bottom. They'll start where you left off—because you did the work.

And you did it fucking beautifully.

Affirmation to end this chapter:

I am worthy as fuck.

Chapter 13: This Is What Love Looks Like (After The Wreckage)

"Turns out, love isn't fireworks-it's consistency, honesty, and not needing a therapist after date night."

Because if you can't handle my sass, my healing, and my boundaries—you're not my person.

There was a time when the idea of love made me want to throw up in my mouth a little. Not because I was bitter (okay, maybe a little), but because I genuinely didn't believe it was meant for me—not real love anyway. Not the kind of love that felt safe. That didn't come with a side of betrayal, silence, manipulation, or "WTF was that?" energy.

After years of disappointment and what I lovingly refer to as a masterclass in dating disasters, I came to the conclusion that love was a scam. A cute little illusion packaged in memes and filtered couples 'selfies. And healing? That was a solo game. The only arms I needed to fall into were my own.

But then something shifted.

Not overnight, not with fairy lights and fireworks. It was gradual. Messy. And started with the scariest damn thing of all: trusting myself.

Because before I could trust someone else with my heart—I had to believe I was finally giving it to the right person.

And surprise: that person wasn't him—it was me.

Let's Back It Up: From Pit bull Mode to Peeling Back Layers

I wasn't exactly a warm and fuzzy open book when this new man walked into my life. In fact, I was more like a heavily padlocked vault with laser tripwires and a guard dog named "Try Me, Bitch."

See, by the time he showed up, I had perfected the art of emotional self-defence. I'd been through the fire—and I'd emerged a little scorched, a lot skeptical, and highly unimpressed by men who claimed they were "different."

And this man? He was too kind. Too thoughtful. Too emotionally intelligent. I didn't trust it. I was waiting for the mask to drop.

He'd tell me sweet things—like how beautiful I looked when I wasn't even trying, or how he noticed that I rubbed my hands when I was anxious—and I'd mentally scan for the red flags like a TSA agent with a trauma detector.

I'd snap. I'd test. I'd go full pit bull over the smallest things. And this man—this actual grown-ass emotionally available man—would pause, breathe, and say something like, "You don't have to fight me."

What the fuck do you mean I don't have to fight?

Fighting was my love language. Because I thought if I wasn't constantly on edge, I'd miss something. That if I let my guard down, I'd be blindsided. Again.

But here's the thing—he didn't take the bait.

Instead of defending himself, he'd get quiet. He'd give me space. He'd say, "I see you're hurt. I'll be here when you're ready to talk."

That's the moment I realized I had no idea what to do with safe love.

The Love I Didn't Know I Deserved

He noticed the things no one ever had—not just the big things, but the tiny details.
Like how I breathe different when I'm stressed.
How I pull away ever so slightly when I feel misunderstood.
How I shut down if I sense judgment before I speak.

He never told me to stop doing any of that.
He didn't try to fix me.
He just saw me.

Not the curated version of me.
Not the tough girl with the jokes.
Not the mom. Not the brand.
Me.

The girl with the scars.
The woman with the walls.
The soul who was terrified of being abandoned if she got too real.

He peeled back the layers, gently, without prying.
He didn't care how long it took. He wasn't keeping score.
He was just present.
Consistent.
Calm.

I remember the first time I believed him when he said, "I'm not going anywhere."

I didn't say it back.
I just cried.

Not because I was sad.
Because I didn't know that kind of love existed.
And maybe, just maybe, I was worthy of it.

The Rainbows Only Come After the Rain

Don't get it twisted—our story isn't all rainbows and roses.
There were moments we both wanted to give up.
Times when our trauma clashed like thunderclouds.
When he stopped tagging me in all those cutesy posts because I made him feel like it wasn't genuine.

Yep. I did that.

I hurt him—not because I meant to—but because I didn't believe it was real.
I doubted his words. I questioned his actions.
Because every time someone had made me feel special before, it came with strings, manipulation, or a silent countdown to betrayal.

So, when he showed up with kindness?
When he mirrored back everything, I'd always wanted but never trusted?
I told him it was "too much."
That it was "fake."
That he must want something.

And the worst part?
He believed me.

He stopped trying to show love the way he naturally gave it—because I rejected it.

That's the part most people don't talk about.
How we sometimes sabotage the good things.
Not because we're ungrateful.
But because we haven't healed enough to receive them.

Healing With Someone, Not Because of Them

Here's what's different about this man:
He didn't try to heal me.
He just held space while I healed myself.

He didn't tell me to "calm down" when I spiralled.
He asked what I needed.
He didn't say, "You're too much."
He said, "I've got you."

And maybe the biggest shock of all?
When he messed up—he took accountability, without me begging. Without ultimatums.
He recognized it.
He did the work.
He apologized.
And he changed the behaviour.

That's when I realized what real love is.

It's not grand gestures.
It's not being saved.
It's not never arguing.

It's growth.

It's safety.
It's respect.
And it's two people doing the work—together and individually.

Because a healthy relationship isn't two halves making a whole.
It's two whole-ass people showing up every day with open hearts and aligned boundaries.

Love Me Like I Finally Love Myself

Because when you glow from within, the right people don't run—they lean in.
You ever have someone look at you in a way that makes you feel seen in your rawest, most unfiltered form?

That happened to me.

And the wildest part wasn't how he looked at me.
It was what other people started to say when they looked at me.

"You're smiling again.
"That real smile… we haven't seen that in years."
"You seem lighter."
"You're glowing."

And I wasn't wearing a new highlighter or trying out a new skincare routine.
It was because I was finally at peace.

Not because he completed me—fuck that fairy tale bullshit.
But because I had finally stopped abandoning myself.

The People Who Noticed

It wasn't just about him. It was about me—and how I was showing up differently in the world.

My daughter noticed first.
She didn't say it outright—kids rarely do.
But she watched. She watched everything.
And I could feel it, the way she looked at me.
The way she smiled when I laughed, the way she no longer hovered around me when I cried—because I wasn't crying out of breakdown, I was crying from release.

And that hit me deep.

Because when you're healing, especially when you're a mom, you always wonder—am I fucking this up for her?

Am I passing down my pain?

But what I realized is that she wasn't just watching me break—
She was watching me rebuild.

And that was the most powerful thing I could've ever taught her.
Not how to avoid heartbreak.
Not how to never get knocked down.

But how to get up. Every. Single. Time.
How to rise with grace and fire and a middle finger to anything that tried to dim her light.

The Truth About Worthy Love

We romanticize the idea of someone "choosing us."

But that's not the goal. The goal is someone who doesn't flinch when you choose yourself.
Someone who doesn't feel threatened when you say, "That doesn't feel right for me."
Who doesn't manipulate, guilt, or gaslight you for having boundaries.
Someone who respects the standard—and doesn't expect a discount.

Real love won't punish you for evolving.
It will grow with you.

And the craziest part? That kind of love doesn't feel chaotic.
It feels calm.

Like, what's the catch?
Where's the toxicity?
Where's the drama?

There isn't any.

Because when two healed (or healing) people come together, there's space.
Space for honesty.
Space for mistakes.
Space to fuck up, say sorry, and actually mean it.

And that—THAT—is what changes everything.

What He Taught Me (Without Trying To)

This man?
He didn't try to fix me.

He didn't try to complete me.
He didn't try to earn my love by putting on a performance.
He just was.
And that still blows my mind.

He paid attention to the things no one else did.
He remembered the things I said when I thought no one was listening.
He noticed when I rubbed my hands.
He rubbed my back in silence instead of forcing me to talk.

He didn't rush the process.
He let me unfold.

He saw the parts of me that were still afraid to be loved—and he didn't take them personally.
He just stayed.
Not to "prove himself,"
But because love, to him, wasn't a chore.
It was a choice.

And every day, he chose to show up.
Even when I made it hard.
Even when I questioned it.
Even when I was too scared to believe it.

It Was Never About Finding the Right Man

It was about becoming the version of me who could recognize one Because old me, she would've self-sabotaged the shit out of this She would've pushed him away, called him boring, Told her friends, "He's nice, but I'm not sure there's chemistry."

When in reality—nice felt foreign to a nervous system used to chaos.
Healing teaches you to stop confusing intensity for intimacy It helps you see that peace isn't boring—it's safe and you're not broken for craving it. You're just finally healed enough to hold it.

The Glow Up Is Real—But So Is the Responsibility

When you get to this place—this real, raw, grounded place—where you finally know your worth, the game changes. You stop settling for half-love, you stop shrinking to keep people comfortable, you stop making excuses for behaviour that hurts.

But here's the kicker:
You also have to respect their boundaries too, you don't get to bulldoze through someone else's healing, you don't get to demand perfection because you've done the work, you don't get to use your trauma as a license to project.

Love is a two-way street.
It's "I've got me" and "I've got you, it's giving grace, but not tolerating disrespect, it's learning to say "I'm sorry" without shame, and "I need space" without guilt.

And that? That's the kind of love I never thought I'd experience.
Because for the longest time, I didn't think I deserved it.
My Final Lesson? No One Else Is Responsible for Your Happiness

It's a solo mission.

Someone can add to it—hell yes, they can amplify it, they can reflect it back to you like a mirror.
But they're not the source.
Your joy, Your peace, Your glow-up.
That's you, baby.

You lead by example You love yourself so hard, so fully, so unapologetically, that when someone else comes along—they either rise to meet that energy or they get left behind and when you do that?
The right people won't be intimidated.
They'll be inspired.
Because people can only love you to the capacity that you love yourself.
And when you raise the bar?
The real ones won't flinch They'll meet you there—with their own healed hands, open hearts, and no fucking ego.

Closing Words of This Chapter:

**To the women still waiting for love—
Start by choosing you.**

To the ones healing in silence—
Keep going.
To the ones afraid to trust again—
Trust yourself first, and to the man who finally reminded me what it felt like to be loved without conditions:

Thank you for showing me I wasn't too much—
I was just finally in the right hands.

Affirmation:

"I am worthy as fuck."

Chapter 14: Burn The Rulebook, Rewire The Truth.

"Your healing doesn't have to look holy to be valid"

Burn the Bridge, Bitch—We're Not Going Back

Let's get one thing straight before we go any further, This chapter is not a pity party.
It's a fucking funeral for the version of you that kept apologizing, shrinking, explaining, begging, tolerating, breaking, and bleeding for people who were never qualified to hold your heart.

You've made it through the damn trenches, babe.
And if you're still reading this book after everything we've unpacked—
the toxic exes, the identity breakdowns, the shattered crowns, the chronic self-abandonment masked as "love"—
then you already know this isn't just a book.
It's a fucking resurrection.

Let's rewind.

First, There Was Chapter 1: Hoover This, Bitch

We kicked this journey off by dragging some skeletons out of the high school closet- and setting them on fire.
Chapter 1 was about the nickname that tried to define me "Hoover" A rumour. A blowjob I Never gave A label I didn't ask for, and how it followed me like a curse for twenty fucking years- until one day I decided to own the damn name and flip the script.
This wasn't just about slut shamming or some bitch at a party reliving her glory days. This was my first taste of what it feels like to be shames into silence…and what it takes to rip your voice back.
Because the truth is: **I didn't suck dick- but I did suck down a lot of shame.**
Not any more

Chapter 1 was mu first rebellion, my first "Fuck You" to the story they wrote for me. And I was just getting started....

Then Came Chapter 2: The Relationship That Broke You
That was the chapter where we talked about the one—the man who cracked your sense of self wide open and danced in the wreckage. The one you kept taking back because you thought he was home. But baby, he was a fucking war zone with Wi-Fi.
You confused chaos for passion.
You called the silent treatment "space."
You turned crumbs into gourmet meals just to feel fed.

And when it ended, you didn't even feel relief. You felt shame.
Because you gave him everything—and he gave you absolutely nothing but a new playlist of breakup songs and a reason to start therapy.

Chapter 3: Trophy Wife, Burned Alive
The pretty little picture you painted—the marriage, the title, the house, the role? It cracked like a cheap ceramic mug when life hit you with the truth: you were drowning in expectations, not love.You kept the house clean but lost yourself in the process. You held it together for the kids, the community, the illusion.
But behind closed doors, you were begging someone—anyone—to see that the woman in the mirror was dying for someone to ask if she was okay.

Spoiler alert: that someone had to be you.

Chapter 4: The Silent Shame of a "Broken" Body

This chapter punched people in the gut—and it fucking should.
Because nobody talks about how infertility shatters your identity as a woman. The grief. The rage. The questions like: "What did I do wrong?" "Why me?" "Am I broken?"

And still—you showed up. You carried hope like it was a job.
You stitched together a smile when your insides were unraveling.
You took needles, hormones, disappointment, and whispered prayers—and you got back up every time.

If that's not divine feminine power, I don't know what the fuck is.

Chapter 5: Nice Guys, Red Flags, and Red Wine
We talked about dating after divorce, single mom life, and the damn circus act of trying to find love when you're still patching bullet holes from your last "forever."
You met the "nice" guys—who were just as toxic, but with a better filter.
You saw the red flags, but you were tired. So you poured another glass, hoped for the best, and cried when it crashed. Again.

Because even after all that healing, there was still a part of you whispering:

"Am I too broken to be loved?"

No, babe. You were just too whole for people who didn't know how to love without control.

Chapter 6: The Perception you belong to me Lets be clear: this wasn't love
I thought it was a casual hook up- a no string attached Booty call situation.
He thought he owned me
What started as booty call turned into a nightmare. The stalking, the obsession, the control. He held joe down, brought bullets to my house, threatened to kill me and destroyed any sense of safety I had left, and while he only got a year behind bars. I got hit with a lifetime of triggers, fear and PTSD.
This chapter wasn't about heartbreak. It was about survival.
It was about the terror of being hunted by someone who believed I was his property- Someone who. Mistook access to my body as a claim to my life.
This wasn't my fault. I didn't, ask for it. But I did rise from it- that makes me dangerous in the best fucking way
Chapter: 7, 8, 9... Whew. The Narcissist Era
This whole goddamn saga deserves its own Netflix series. We unpacked it all:
- *The love bombing.*
- *The gaslighting.*
- *The fucking silent treatment that felt like psychological warfare.*
- *The "you're not my mother" bullshit when all you wanted was basic-ass communication.*
- *The way they twisted your words, used your kindness against you, and made you feel like the crazy one while they played victim in their head.*

Let's call it what it is:
Narcissistic abuse is a slow erasure of the self and you barely realized it was happening until you looked in the mirror and couldn't recognize the woman staring back.
But guess what?
You survived. You made it out. You're here.

And we are never, ever going back.

Chapter 10: The Aftermath — "I Am Not Enough"
This chapter gutted people. You know why?

Because that phrase—"I am not enough"—is the root of every toxic decision we've ever made.
Every time you stayed when you should've left.
Every time you shrunk so someone else could shine.
Every time you apologized for shit that wasn't your fault.
Every time you over gave, overworked, over-explained, and over-extended yourself until you couldn't even remember what you wanted or who the hell you were.

It wasn't because you were weak.
It's because you were conditioned to believe that love is something you earn.

But in Chapter 10, we flipped the script.
We called bullshit on the whole "fill his cup first" narrative.
You can't pour from an empty cup—and guess what? You never fucking had to.

Because love isn't a job.
It's not a reward for loyalty.
It's not a prize for self-abandonment.
And your worth isn't a goddamn receipt someone needs to validate.

Chapter 11: The Wellness Trap
Now this one? It stung. Because wellness culture loves to market to women who feel like they're not enough. Green juices. Face rollers. Detox teas. $200 yoga mats. Meditation apps that charge you monthly to "find your peace."

Meanwhile, you're crying into a matcha smoothie wondering why your life still feels like a dumpster fire.

Here's the truth:
Self-worth doesn't come in a 30-day reset plan.
You can't bio-hack your way out of trauma.
And you sure as hell can't "positive vibe" your way through unprocessed pain.

You needed something deeper. Something real.
So you stopped chasing the next fix and started doing the real work.
You stopped obsessing over your waistline and started focusing on your boundaries.
You stopped counting macros and started counting the ways you betrayed yourself to be liked.

And that, my love, is when the healing actually began.

Chapter 12: Mom Guilt is a Lying Bitch

Now if Chapter 12 didn't make every mom reading this cry in the pantry—I don't know what will.

You opened up about the raw, unfiltered guilt that follows us like a damn shadow.
The lies we tell ourselves:

"I'm ruining her childhood."
"She'll need therapy because of me."
"I'm not doing enough."

But here's what made this chapter so fucking powerful:
You didn't pretend to be perfect.

You owned the mess. You embraced the chaos.
And you showed us that breaking cycles doesn't mean being flawless—it means being honest.

You let your daughter watch you fall apart...
And then she watched you rebuild.
And even if that journey was jagged and slow—you were showing her something more powerful than perfection.
You were showing her what healing looks like in real time.
And baby, that's fucking generational wealth.

Chapter 13: The Real Thing
This chapter was the plot twist.
The I made it out alive and learned to love again chapter.

It wasn't a fairytale. It wasn't a Nicholas Sparks moment.
It was better.

Because you didn't find someone to complete you; you found someone who saw you.

The girl who was once called "too much"?
He called her magic.

The woman who rubbed her hands when she was anxious.
He noticed. He cared.

You didn't have to beg him to show up.
You didn't have to teach him how to respect you.
And when you fucked up?
He didn't weaponize it. He held space for it. Then grew through it—with you.

That, babe, is what real love looks like.
Not perfect. Not Instagram-worthy.

But rooted in growth, accountability, space, and showing the fuck up—especially on the hard days.

Now We're Here.

You've walked through fire.
You've cried on bathroom floors.
You've answered late-night texts you knew you shouldn't.
You've lost yourself. Found yourself. Lost yourself again.
You've screamed at the universe and begged for signs.
You've stayed too long. Left too soon. Started over more times than you can count.
And you're still fucking standing.

Actually—scratch that.
You're not just standing.
You're rising.

You're no longer looking for permission.
You're no longer waiting for closure.
You're no longer apologizing for the space you take up or the truth you speak.

This is the chapter where the old you dies—and you cremate that bitch with glitter, sass, and a fireproof pair of heels.

You're not broken.
You're not "too much."
You're not the mistakes you made when you didn't know better.
You're not the pain they caused you.

You're not the version of you who let red flags become home decor.

You're a whole-ass woman.
Worthy. Wild. Wounded, maybe—but walking forward anyway.

And if there's one thing this entire book has taught you—it's this:

You never needed to be chosen to matter.
You never needed to be perfect to be loved.
And you never, ever needed to shrink to survive.

I am Worthy AF

Let's Flip The Fucking Script

This is the part where the victim dies and the main character rises - pen in hand, middle finger raised, rewriting everything they said you couldn't be.

Chapter 15: The Childhood Wounds They Said Weren't That Bad

"'I wasn't just teasing.' It was trauma with a smile"

When Your Inner Child Becomes the Loudest Bitch in the Room

Let's just cut the crap for a second and tell the goddamn truth: most of us didn't grow up in safe, emotionally supportive, "my feelings matter" environments. We grew up in houses where survival looked like silence. Where crying got you labeled dramatic, asking questions got you the side-eye, and God forbid you said no—you were either grounded, guilt-tripped, or gaslit.

And then we wonder why we grow up into adults who can't say no, who apologize for existing, who bend over backwards for love that doesn't even meet us halfway. Here's the real talk your therapist might gently guide you into… but I'm kicking the fucking door down with it:

Your childhood was not your fault.
But healing it? That's your responsibility.

I don't care if you had a "decent" childhood and your parents "meant well." Trauma isn't about how bad it looks—it's about how bad it felt. Emotional neglect is still neglect. Being told "you're too sensitive" is still invalidation. Being made to feel like your worth depended on your grades, your weight, your obedience, or your ability to make everyone else comfortable? That shit stays buried deep. Until it explodes.

Let me tell you about mine. Not the darkest, most dramatic moment—but the sneaky one. The one that didn't feel like trauma but fucked me up for decades.

I was nine. My report card came home with a C in math. Now, I'd been struggling—real shit, long division felt like black magic. I was already embarrassed. I handed it over to my dad like it was a loaded weapon. He didn't yell. He didn't beat me. He just raised his eyebrows, sighed, and said, "You're smarter than this." That's it. That fucking sentence.

And my brain? It didn't just hear disappointment. It translated it into: You're not enough. You're only lovable when you're performing. Try harder. Be better. Do more.

Welcome to the first moment my inner child decided she needed to hustle for worth. That perfectionism? That constant need to prove myself. That relentless people-pleasing? It didn't come from nowhere. It was built one "not good enough" moment at a time.

Why We Don't Heal (and Why That Ends Now)

Let me break this down for you: your unhealed childhood wounds didn't just vanish because you turned 18. They just got better at wearing lipstick and pretending everything's fine.

We think healing our inner child is some woo-woo, incense-burning, finger-painting bullshit. And yeah, sometimes it is finger painting—rage painting, if you're doing it right. But most of the time, healing looks like finally saying, "Fuck that. I deserved better."

You ever wonder why you shrink when someone raises their voice? Why you feel guilty for resting? Why you chase unavailable people and call it "chemistry"? Why you feel like you're too much and never enough at the same damn time?

That's your inner child screaming from the back seat:
See me.
Hear me.
Love me the way no one else did."

But instead of listening, we silence her with wine, TikTok scrolling, or another situationship that looks like Daddy Issues in a Snapback.

Here's the kicker: we're not just healing our childhood. We're unlearning how we survived it. And that's messy as fuck.

The "Good Girl" Programming That Made You a Doormat

Let's talk about how society (and some of our sweet-but-toxic families) trained us to be digestible. To be "good."
And let's be honest—"good" usually meant:
- *Be quiet.*
- *Be nice.*
- *Don't argue.*
- *Don't have boundaries.*
- *Don't embarrass us.*

In other words: Don't be a real fucking human with needs.

And this programming didn't magically disappear when we grew up. It followed us into jobs where we overwork and undercharge. Into friendships where we're the unpaid therapist. Into relationships where we confuse control with love.

Being a "good girl" taught you that saying yes made you lovable. But guess what? Being agreeable doesn't make you worthy. It makes you exhausted.

The Shitty Things You Believed About Yourself (That Weren't Even Yours)

Let me drop a truth grenade right here:

If your parents never felt good enough, they probably raised you in a way that made you feel not good enough too.

Maybe your mom was raised to believe her body was something to fix, hide, or criticize—so she passed that shit down to you, complimenting your weight loss more than your wins. Maybe your dad never learned emotional regulation, so anger was the only language he spoke. Or maybe they both loved you, but they didn't know how to show it in a way that landed.

Generational trauma isn't always violence. Sometimes it's silence. It's shame. Its sacrifice wrapped up in martyrdom and toxic loyalty. It's "We don't talk about that." It's "Don't cry or I'll give you something to cry about." It's never being asked how you feel—just told how to act.

We inherit that shit like family recipes. Only instead of banana bread, we get abandonment issues and trust problems.

And Let's Not Forget School: A.K.A. The Hunger Games for Self-Worth

If your family didn't do the damage, school probably picked up the slack.
Bullying? Check.
Teacher favouritism? Check.
Gym class trauma? Double fucking check.

How many of us were made to feel stupid, slow, awkward, ugly, or "too much" by the very place that was supposed to help us grow?

One wrong answer on a test and you were "dumb." One awkward puberty stage and you were "gross." One moment of standing up for yourself and you were "a bitch."

And here we are, decades later, still trying to rewrite the script.

Reparenting the Inner Bitch Who Just Wanted to Feel Safe

Alright babe, grab your journal and your emotional first-aid kit, because this is where the real healing begins.

You've faced the truth—your childhood wasn't all sunshine and fruit snacks. But now what? Now comes the part they don't talk about enough. The part that's messy, uncomfortable, and weirdly beautiful:

You get to reparent yourself.
Yep. You. Grown-ass, badass, tired-as-fuck you.

Because the truth is, we've all been walking around in adult bodies, reacting from a 7-year-old mindset. A kid who didn't feel safe. A teen who just wanted approval. A little girl who needed someone to say, "You're not crazy. You're hurting. And that makes sense."

Here's the kicker no one warned us about: when you start healing, it doesn't feel good. It feels like grief. Like pulling the rug out from under the life you thought was normal and realizing, holy shit, none of this was okay.

Healing Isn't a Spa Day. It's a War Zone With Throw Pillows.

Reparenting isn't about blaming your parents forever. It's about saying: "You did the best you could with what you had.
But now I'm doing better—with what I have."

It means you become the voice you needed. You stop looking outside for validation and start giving it to yourself. You create safety within your own nervous system. You learn to sit with your feelings instead of swallowing them like expired tequila.

Here's what that can actually look like (spoiler: it's not cute Instagram quotes and bubble baths):

- *You wake up with anxiety and instead of scrolling TikTok, you ask yourself, "What do I need right now?"*
- *You say no to dinner with that friend who drains you, even if you feel guilty.*
- *You cry over shit that happened 20 years ago and stop gaslighting yourself about it.*
- *You apologize to your inner child for making her feel like she had to earn love.*
- *You let yourself rest without earning it first.*

- *You start saying, "I love you" in the mirror even when it feels awkward as hell.*

This shit is radical. Because when you reparent yourself, you're doing what generations of women weren't allowed to do: you're healing out loud. You're giving your daughter, your friends, and even your fucking Instagram followers permission to do the same.

Let's Talk Triggers: Not Everything Is About Him, Sis

You ever get triggered by something small—like someone interrupting you or your partner not texting back—and suddenly you're spiralling like it's a goddamn Lifetime movie?

Yeah. That's not about them. That's about then.

When your body feels unsafe, your brain hits the emergency eject button and launches you back into childhood. Suddenly, you're 8 years old again, sitting at the kitchen table, being ignored. Or you're 15 and someone's mocking your voice. And your nervous system? She doesn't know the difference between then and now. She just knows, this hurts. This feels familiar. Danger ahead.

That's why healing isn't logical. It's biological.
And that's also why you need to stop judging yourself for overreacting and start asking, "What part of me is still unhealed?"

Because when you know where it's coming from, you can stop blaming yourself for the explosion—and start disarming the bomb.

Dear Inner Child: I'm So Fucking Sorry

Let's write her a letter. I'm serious. Get a pen. (Yes, you. The grown-ass woman reading this like she's not crying a little already.)

Write to that little girl who felt like too much. Or not enough. Or both.

Say:

"I'm sorry I didn't listen when you were tired.
I'm sorry I forced you to smile through pain.
I'm sorry I chased love that didn't even know how to see you.
But I see you now. I hear you. I'm here. And I've got you."

That's it. That's how healing starts.
It's not a finish line. It's not a TED Talk moment. It's a whisper. A promise.

You deserved softness. You deserved boundaries. You deserved safety and joy and a fucking gold star for surviving what no child should've had to navigate.

Now, you give it to yourself.

Healing Means You Get to Choose Now

Here's the power move of the century:

When you heal your childhood, you stop living from it.
You stop choosing partners who trigger your abandonment wounds.
You stop over-explaining your boundaries like you need permission.
You stop shrinking to fit into the role someone else wrote for you.

Instead, you write your own damn story.

You show your kids that they can speak up and still be loved You build relationships based on truth instead of performance, You stop performing for applause and start living for peace.

And that's what makes you Worthy AF.
Not perfection. Not pretending. But presence.

You're here.
You're healing.
And that shit is holy.

Your Worthy AF Healing Homework:

7 Journal Prompts to Rewire Your Inner Child's Beliefs

1. What did I need to hear as a child that I never did?

2. What parts of myself do I hide because they weren't accepted growing up?

3. When was the first time I remember feeling "not enough"?

_____
_____
_____
_____
_____
_____
_____
_____
_____
_____
_____
_____
_____
_____
_____
_____
_____
_____
_____
_____
_____
_____
_____
_____
_____
_____
_____
_____
_____

4. What patterns am I repeating that came from childhood coping mechanisms?

5. How do I show love to everyone except myself?

6. What would my 8-year-old self think of me now?

7. If I could give my inner child one promise, what would it be?

Breakthrough Exercise:

The "Rewrite the Scene" Practice

Pick one memory from childhood that still stings. Write it down in full detail—the sights, the feelings, the words.

Then? Rewrite it.
Become the parent, the protector, the advocate you needed in that moment.

What would they say to you? How would they hold you? What would change?

Do this every week. And watch how you stop living like a victim of the past and start stepping into the author of your future.

Chapter 16: Healing The Mirror: Rebuilding The Self Trust

"You can't love yourself if you don't believe in yourself"

The Internship from Hell You Never Signed Up For

There's a special place in emotional hell for the relationships where you didn't just love someone— you project managed their life. You weren't just the girlfriend, wife, or partner. No, babe, you were the therapist, motivational coach, sex goddess, mommy figure, and the poor bastard's personal saviour wrapped in Spanx and self-doubt.

Let's not sugarcoat this. You took on a full-time emotional labor role with zero pay, no benefits, and a boss who probably couldn't even spell "empathy."

You cooked the meals, sent the check-in texts, read the self-help books, scheduled the therapy appointments (for him, of course), wrote him long messages explaining how he made you feel (which he never read), and got rewarded with... what? Ghosting? Gaslighting? Or just plain old emotional constipation?

Let's call this what it was:
The Fix-Him Phase.
Also known as:
"I believed in your potential harder than I believed in myself."

Welcome to the Delulu Era: Where You Dated a Damn Project

There was a time you saw his brokenness and thought, "I can help him heal."
You weren't naive. You were conditioned. You grew up thinking love meant sacrifice, that if you just loved someone hard enough, you could unlock their better version like a damn video game.

So you stayed.
Through the mood swings, the blame games, the "I'm just not ready" speeches.
You became fluent in the language of excuses: "He had a rough childhood."
"He's just stressed from work."
"He doesn't mean it."

Let me hit you with a truth bomb, babe:
You cannot love someone into emotional maturity.

Read that again.

And then put it on a T-shirt, hang it on your mirror, and tattoo it on your damn soul. Because what you were doing That wasn't love, That was codependency dressed up in commitment issues and a fear of abandonment. You were the band-aid, not the cure. And baby, you are not a band-aid—you are a fucking breakthrough.

But He Had So Much Potential....
Ah yes, potential.
The romantic equivalent of a Ponzi scheme.

Let me say this louder for the people in the back:
Potential doesn't mean a damn thing if it never becomes action, You fell in love with what could be instead of what was And that shit's dangerous Because when you're high on the fantasy, you start excusing the reality.

He ignores your texts? "He's just overwhelmed."
He doesn't open up? "He's not used to feeling safe."
He talks to his ex behind your back? "He's confused."

Babe. He's not confused. He's comfortable.

And you? You were exhausted, Because trying to heal someone who doesn't even believe they're broken is a never-ending mind-fuck that'll drain your soul and your skincare budget.

You know what it feels like?
Like screaming into a void, begging to be seen while simultaneously shrinking yourself to be palatable.
You gave up your boundaries, your time, your peace—all in the name of love. But it wasn't love.
It was fear….Of being alone, Of not being chosen, Of failing at the one thing society told you should come naturally—making it work.

"Fixing Him" Was Really About Fixing You

Here's the spicy plot twist:
You weren't trying to fix him. You were trying to fix the part of you that believed love had to be earned. That
if you could just be enough—
calm enough,
pretty enough,
understanding enough—then maybe someone would finally stay.

You tried to be the solution to his pain because no one ever gave you permission to tend to your own.
And now?
You're waking up, You're realizing that it wasn't your job to be his emotional dumpster, You were never supposed to set yourself on fire just to keep his inner child warm.

It's time to walk away from the role of emotional janitor.

Not because you don't love him. But because you finally love yourself more.

The Fucked-Up Fairy Tale You Got Sold

Let's call out the conditioning, shall we?

You were raised on fairy tales that glorified self-sacrifice. Cinderella cleaned up everyone's shit for a man with a foot fetish. Ariel literally gave up her voice to chase a guy who'd never heard her speak. Belle fell in love with a hairy narcissist and we called it "romantic."

NO THANK YOU.

Love isn't supposed to hurt more than it heals.
You don't have to "save him." You're not his mom. You're not his mirror., You're not his fucking rehab, You are the whole-ass table, not a support beam for his collapsing ego.

The Emotional Invoice You'll Never Get Paid For (And Why You're Done Paying For It Too)

The Debt You Never Signed Up For (But Paid Anyway)

Here's the thing nobody talks about:

When you date or marry a man who needs fixing, you're racking up emotional debt in silence. It's like charging your soul to a credit card you never applied for, and the interest rate is fucking brutal.

You're fronting all the energy:

- *The pep talks*
- *The forgiveness*
- *The "It's okay, babe" when it clearly was not okay*
- *The I'm-sorry-even-though-you-hurt-me apologies*

And what do you get in return?
A pat on the head? A thank-you text two days late? A man who "means well" but forgets your birthday and emotionally checks out the second he's uncomfortable?

Here's the wake-up call:
The moment you become the only source of stability in the relationship, you're not a partner—you're a crutch.
And crutches don't get loved.
They get leaned on. Used. Eventually discarded when the limp's gone—or when he finds a newer, shinier model of dependency.
You were never supposed to be his emotional wheelchair, sis.

Resentment: The Rotten Fruit of Emotional Over giving

Let's talk about the slow poison that brews in these relationships: resentment.

At first, you swallow it.
You justify it.
You tell yourself, "He's trying."
But every unreciprocated effort, every dismissed emotion, every time you cried alone…

It adds up.

And one day, you wake up so full of rage you could burn down the whole damn relationship with one sarcastic comment. And honestly? He probably deserves it.

But here's where it gets real:
You can't be mad at someone for continuing to take what you keep giving.

Yup. That stings.
You trained him to believe your love was unconditional—even when it should have come with terms, boundaries, and a fucking user manual.

You were so afraid of losing him, you lost you.

And the resentment wasn't just toward him.
It was toward the version of you that tolerated crumbs, that gaslit herself into staying, that chose potential over peace.

The Real Reason You Stayed (Spoiler: It Wasn't Love)

Let's go deep for a second.

The real reason you stayed wasn't loyalty.
It wasn't love.
It wasn't even hope.
It was familiarity.
You stayed because on some level, that dysfunction felt like home.

Maybe your dad didn't show up. Maybe your mom was emotionally absent. Maybe you were the responsible one since you were seven. Maybe you were praised for being the "good girl," the fixer, the selfless one.

So when a broken man came along who needed saving, your trauma said, "Ah yes, this feels safe. Let's recreate our childhood with a penis involved."

It's dark. It's messy. But it's true.

You didn't choose that relationship from your healed self.
You chose it from your wounded self.
And wounded people don't pick partners—they pick patterns.

When You Stopped Trying to Fix Him, You Started Healing You

Let's get to the part where the main character reclaims her fucking power.

The moment you stopped trying to fix him, something magical happened:
You realized the only project you needed to work on was yourself.
And baby? You crushed it.
You stopped bending over backward to earn love that should've been given freely, You stopped tolerating silence as an answer, You stopped dimming your shine to keep his ego from feeling small, You built boundaries that weren't just fences—they were fucking fortresses, You became the version of yourself you used to cry about becoming.
The woman who doesn't settle. Who doesn't chase. Who doesn't audition for the bare minimum.

You became Worthy AF.

You Don't Need to Be His Everything—Just Your Own

Let me say this straight up:

You're not here to be someone's rehab.
You're not here to be their wake-up call.
You're not the one meant to teach them how to be a decent fucking human.

You deserve a man who meets you where you are. Who doesn't need you to shrink, fix, or heal him first. Someone who's done the damn work—or at least doing it without you dragging his ass through every uncomfortable emotion. You don't need to carry someone, You need someone who walks beside you.

Because love isn't supposed to feel like a second job.
It's supposed to feel like home—not the kind you're trying to escape from.

Final Truth Bomb Before the Journal Prompts

You weren't too much.
You weren't too emotional.
You weren't too intense.
You were just too aware for someone still choosing to live in denial.

The next chapter of your life isn't about proving your worth to anyone else.
It's about finally recognizing that you were never broken. You were just trying to glue together a man who was already choosing to stay shattered.

Let that sink in.

CHAPTER 16: HEALING TOOLKIT

"The Emotional Invoice You'll Never Get Paid For (And Why You're Done Paying For It Too)"

7 Journal Prompts to Un-fuck Your Fix-Him Pattern:

1. What did I believe I had to earn in love that should've been unconditional?
(Dig deep—affection, attention, validation, safety... what did you chase instead of receive?

2. Where did I learn that love means self-sacrifice? Who taught me that narrative? (Childhood, church, TV, a parent? Call it out so you can cancel the damn subscription.)

_____
_____
_____
_____
_____
_____
_____
_____
_____
_____
_____
_____
_____
_____
_____
_____
_____
_____
_____
_____
_____
_____
_____
_____
_____
_____

3. How did trying to fix him distract me from fixing myself?
(What were you avoiding—your own healing, loneliness, fear of failure?)

4. What parts of me did I silence or shrink to keep that relationship afloat?
(Be specific—your opinions, your goals, your intuition, your sex drive?)

5. What red flags did I excuse, and what did I tell myself to justify them?
(Write the lies. Then write the truth.)

6. How do I show up for others in ways I don't show up for myself?
(And how can you flip that starting TODAY?)

7. What does a healthy, reciprocal relationship actually look like for me?
(Describe it without a single reference to "potential.")

Cord-Cutting Ritual: Energetically Let Him the Fuck Go

You don't need sage or moonlight (but hey, go wild). Here's a no-fluff Worthy AF version:

Step 1: Write a goodbye letter.
Say what you never said. Write the rage, the grief, the I-should've-left-sooner.

Step 2: Read it out loud.
Yes, out loud. Alone. With ugly tears and no holding back.

Step 3: Burn it.
Safely. Over a sink. Outside. Watch that shit turn to ash. He doesn't get to live in your nervous system rent-free anymore.

Step 4: Say this out loud:

**"I am not your fixer. I am not your rehab. I am not your mother.
I release the weight of your healing from my shoulders.
I call all my energy back to me—clean, clear, and complete."**

"I am Worthy AF—and I don't chase crumbs when I deserve the whole fucking feast."

Worthy AF Boundary Blueprint:

Here's the new rules of engagement for your future love life:

- *If I have to guess where I stand, I'm sitting the fuck down—alone.*
- *If my nervous system doesn't feel safe, I'm out.*
- *If the vibe is "fix me," I politely decline the DIY project.*
- *If love doesn't come with respect, accountability, and effort—it's not love. It's manipulation.*

Your Reminder:

You don't need to be a softer version of yourself to be loved.

You don't need to be less assertive, less loud, less emotional, less opinionated.

You just need to be you Fully. Boldly. Worthy AF.

Let this be the last chapter where you water someone else's garden while your own soul is bone fucking dry.

Affirmation to end this chapter:
"I am not a fixer. I am the fucking fire.

I am Worthy as Fuck."

Chapter 17: The Betrayal Was Never About You (But Healing Always Is)

"Cheating says more about their wounds than my worth"

Because you can't bleed out from someone else's wound and call it love.

Let's rip the fucking Band-Aid off right away, shall we?
Infidelity, Betrayal, Ghosts of relationships past that still haunt the fuck out of you.
This chapter? This is the deep, soul-stitched, rage-drenched part of the story where we stop pretending that being cheated on means you weren't good enough.

Because spoiler alert: it was never about you. And holy shit, that's a hard pill to swallow when you're laying in bed at 3 a.m. replaying every conversation, every outfit, every missed blowjob like it's a courtroom drama and you're both judge and defendant.

Let's go back for a second.

When betrayal hits—whether it's a one-night stand, emotional cheating, secret DMs, or a fucking double life—it's like someone hit the emergency brake on your nervous system while dragging your heart down a gravel road.

And your first thought?
"Why wasn't I enough?"

Let me be crystal fucking clear:
You could've been a lingerie-wearing, meal-prepping, sex goddess who hyped him up like a TED Talk and made his favourite sandwich on homemade sourdough with a blowjob on the side—
He still would've cheated if he was going to cheat.
Why?

Because cheating isn't about you. It's about them,
It's about their wounds.,Their self-loathing. Their lack of discipline,Their need to feel powerful, validated, and in control because they're too cowardly to sit with their own goddamn pain.

But you?

You're the one who ends up questioning your worth like it's some thrift store bargain.
You start analyzing every second:
- *Maybe if I didn't gain weight...*
- *Maybe if I wasn't so emotional...*
- *Maybe if I gave him more sex...*

Bitch, NO.

Let's be fucking honest: if a man cheats on you because you gained ten pounds or because you're emotionally intelligent, he wasn't a man—he was a scared little boy using your body as a shield from his own demons.

Here's what no one talks about:
Infidelity isn't just a sexual betrayal.
It's a soul violation.
Because we don't just mourn the loss of the relationship—we mourn who we were before it broke us. Before we started doubting every instinct. Before we forgot how to trust ourselves.

And fuck, that's the real tragedy, isn't it?

We stop trusting ourselves.

That was my biggest realization after betrayal—I didn't have a partner problem. I had a self-trust problem.

I wasn't afraid they would cheat again.
I was afraid I wouldn't see it coming.
I was afraid I'd ignore the red flags again.
I was afraid I'd gaslight myself and call it loyalty.

Because betrayal doesn't just make you hate them—it makes you doubt you and if we don't heal that, we carry it into the next thing. And the next. And the next.

Like emotional herpes.

Let me tell you something that hit me like a truck during one of my own therapy sessions (shout out to my psychotherapist who looked like a kindergarten teacher but came with sniper-level truth bombs):

She said,

"You're not afraid of being betrayed again.
You're afraid of not listening to yourself again."

Read that again.

Betrayal makes us feel stupid, Not just sad. Not just heartbroken, But fucking stupid.

Like we should've known.
Like we missed something.
Like we handed someone the scissors and asked why we're bleeding.

But guess what?

That's what manipulators do.
They're not always evil, but they are damaged.
And unhealed people hurt people.
Just like I hurt people when I was unhealed.

And yep—I'll own that shit too.

I projected my pain onto others. I've questioned good men. I've tried to make someone chase me just to prove I was lovable. I've created chaos just to test their commitment.

Why?

Because I hadn't forgiven the man who betrayed me—and worse, I hadn't forgiven myself for letting it happen.

But you don't heal by punishing the next man for the last one's crimes.
You heal by owning your part in abandoning yourself.
And fuck, that's hard.

But it's freedom.

So let's break this all the way down in the next part: what betrayal does to your identity, how it sneaks into your next relationship, and why reclaiming your self-worth isn't about becoming "better" for someone else—it's about remembering you were never the problem in the first place.

The Delusion That Broke You

Let's talk about the kind of betrayal that doesn't just hurt—it rewires you. The kind that makes you question your entire reality. The kind that fucks with your sense of truth so deeply that you can't tell the difference between your intuition and your anxiety anymore.

That's what betrayal does. It doesn't just break your heart—it breaks your self-trust. And here's the real kicker: when you don't trust yourself, you've got nothing.

Let me say that again louder for the people in the back: When you don't trust yourself, you've got nothing. Not your gut. Not your decisions. Not your worth. You question everything. Every text. Every delay. Every silence. And then you gaslight yourself harder than he ever could.

"Maybe I'm just overreacting."
"He said it's not a big deal, so maybe I'm being dramatic."
"If I hadn't nagged, he wouldn't have stayed out."
"He said I was crazy—and maybe I am."

You know what that is? Delusional thinking disguised as logic. That's what we do when we're trying to make sense of something senseless. When the person we trusted most ripped out our emotional spine and left us crawling through the shards.

Here's the truth no one told you: It's not your job to prevent someone from betraying you. It's your job to believe yourself when you feel something's off.

But when you've been cheated on—emotionally, physically, mentally—your brain doesn't just file it away under "that was messed up." No. It stores it under "what did I do wrong?"

Because betrayal makes you believe it was your fault. And society doesn't fucking help.

He cheated? Well, were you giving him enough attention?
He left? Were you nagging too much?
He lied? Were you too demanding?
He pulled away? Were you just too emotional?

Fuck. That. Shit.

Let me be clear. If someone betrays you, that's a reflection of their character, not your worth.
But knowing that and believing that are two very different things. And for years, I couldn't believe it. I carried the shame like a fucking backpack full of bricks. Every time I tried to move forward, the voice in my head whispered, "But what if it was you? What if you were the problem?"

And because I didn't trust myself, I stayed. I tried harder. I made myself smaller. I stopped asking questions because I didn't want to be "too much." I stayed silent to keep the peace. I became a watered-down version of myself so he wouldn't leave. Spoiler alert: he still left.

Because that's the thing. You can shrink yourself into nothingness, and if someone wants to cheat, lie, or ghost you—they still will. You can be the most supportive, ride-or-die, lunch-packing, ass-clapping queen, and if a man is committed to being a coward, no amount of loyalty is going to change that.

And yet... we blame ourselves.

Why?

Because it's easier to believe we did something wrong than it is to face the terrifying truth that someone we loved chose to hurt us—and we were powerless to stop it.

Powerlessness. That's the wound betrayal leaves behind. And when you don't know how to process that, you start doing something even more dangerous: you start trying to control the uncontrollable.

You become hyper-vigilant. You overthink every interaction. You reread messages. You dissect tones. You start testing people to see if they'll hurt you too. And when they fail your test—even a little—you say, "See? I knew it. I can't trust anyone."

But that's not intuition, babe. That's trauma in a trench coat.

That's what happens when your self-worth gets tangled up in someone else's dysfunction. You start trying to solve a puzzle that was never yours. And in the process, you lose sight of the one person you do have power over—you.

Let me get brutally honest here: The longer you try to decode their betrayal, the longer you delay your healing.

You don't need closure.
You don't need to know "why."
You don't need to understand their trauma, their childhood, their mommy issues, or their Zodiac sign.

You need to say, "They chose to hurt me. That's all I need to know."

You don't need to justify it.
You don't need to make it make sense.
You just need to believe yourself enough to walk away.

Because here's the hardest pill to swallow—and the most freeing truth you'll ever hear:

They didn't break you. You just forgot who the fuck you were.

Let that sit for a second.

You forgot that you're the storm, not the debris.
You forgot that you've survived worse.
You forgot that being betrayed doesn't make you less worthy—it makes you human.

And now... now it's time to come back home to yourself.

THE COMEBACK ISN'T CUTE. IT'S MESSY AS FUCK.

Let's not romanticize this. Healing after betrayal isn't a bubble bath and a "Self-Care Sunday" Post. It's ugly. It's rage and silence and crying on the kitchen floor because your body remembers the pain before your brain does.

It's journaling and rewriting the same sentence 37 times until it finally feels real, it's learning to eat again without a pit in your stomach, it's rebuilding your nervous system from scratch because every ding of your phone still gives you anxiety.

It's screaming into a pillow and then apologizing to your dog for scaring the shit out of him, It's real. It's raw. And it's absolutely worth it.

Because every time you choose yourself again, your worth gets a little louder.

Every time you delete his number and don't redownload it from your brain's trauma file, you grow.

Every time you say, "I deserve better"—and mean it—you get closer to being her.

The version of you that no longer flinches at love.
The version of you that knows her own patterns and calls herself out on them.
The version of you that doesn't beg for crumbs because she remembers she was born the whole damn loaf.

STOP REPEATING THE SAME PATTERNS, SIS.

Let me break the cycle for you. Right here, right now.

If you don't trust yourself, you will always pick the same kind of person. Different name. Different face. Same fucking story.

You'll keep repeating the cycle because deep down, your subconscious is still trying to "get it right" with someone just like them—so you can finally feel worthy. But you don't earn your worth by fixing broken people. You reclaim your worth by walking away from what breaks you. That's the rewrite. That's the shift. That's the exit from the trauma carousel.

Because you can't outrun the pain. But you can outgrow it, and when you do? Oh babe, your glow-up will burn every bridge they ever walked across to fuck with you. You'll shine so bright they'll need shades just to stalk your stories.

Rebuild That Shit—One "I Am" at a Time

You don't heal from betrayal by pretending it didn't hurt, you don't get over it—you get through it and if you're anything like me, when the dust finally settled, you didn't even know who the fuck you were anymore.

But here's the truth that saved me:
You don't have to know exactly who you are.
You just have to stop believing the bullshit story that betrayal wrote for you. That story that says you're too much, too emotional, not enough, too broken, too whatever. Burn it. Then take out a pen and rewrite the story in your own damn handwriting.

EXERCISE 1: Burn the Bullshit Story

Write the story betrayal told you. Be honest. Be brutal.
- *"I'm not enough."*
- *"I'll always be left."*
- *"I can't trust anyone."*
- *"I'm hard to love."*
- Now light that shit on fire. (Safely, please.)

- *As it burns, say out loud:*
  This story doesn't belong to me. I release it. I reclaim the truth.

EXERCISE 2: The "I Am" Rewire Ritual

Let's talk about those little two words that hold BIG fucking power: "I am."

I know it sounds cheesy. I thought it was some Pinterest, bubble-bath, boss-babe nonsense too. But this? This changed me. Because when I couldn't trust anyone else—I needed to learn to trust myself.

Here's the exact ritual that rebuilt me when I was at rock bottom:

Every Morning:
- Before checking your phone.
- Before getting sucked into the chaos.
- Before responding to anyone else's energy.

Do this:
1. Open your journal.
2. Write at least 3 "I Am" statements—even if you don't believe a single one yet.

Start here if you're stuck:
- *I am worthy of love.*
- *I am safe in my body.*
- *I am learning to trust myself again.*
- *I am not what they did to me.*
- *I am not crazy—I was gaslit.*
- *I am healing.*
- *I am enough even when I doubt it.*

- *I am done settling for less than I deserve.*
- *I am building a life I won't need to escape from.*
- *I am no longer available for emotional chaos.*
3. Say them out loud.
4. Look in the mirror and repeat the one that feels the hardest to believe. That's your nervous system's weak spot. That's the one that needs rewiring the most.
5. Write one of your "I Am" statements on your mirror in lipstick or whiteboard marker.

Because when you see it every time you brush your teeth?

That's not woo-woo.

That's neuroscience.

You're creating new neural pathways. New beliefs. New truths And even if it starts with "I don't feel this yet," it will become your truth if you keep showing the fuck up.

JOURNAL PROMPTS TO HEAL FROM BETRAYAL

Take these slowly. One a day if you need to. But write like your life depends on it—because your self-worth does.

1. What beliefs about myself did betrayal create? Are they actually true?

2. What red flags did I ignore, and why did I ignore them?

3. What do I wish I had done differently—and how can I show myself compassion for not knowing then what I know now?

4. When did I stop trusting myself? What did I need in that moment that I didn't get?

_____
_____
_____
_____
_____
_____
_____
_____
_____
_____
_____
_____
_____
_____
_____
_____
_____
_____
_____
_____
_____
_____
_____
_____
_____
_____
_____
_____

5. What boundaries did I need back then that I now know are non-negotiable?

_____
_____
_____
_____
_____
_____
_____
_____
_____
_____
_____
_____
_____
_____
_____
_____
_____
_____
_____
_____
_____
_____
_____
_____
_____
_____
_____

6. Who do I become when I don't trust myself? How does she show up in relationships?

___

7. What will I no longer tolerate in love, life, and friendships? And what new standard am I setting for how I want to be loved?

WORTHY AF AFFIRMATIONS TO BLAST THE TRAUMA LOOP

Stick these to your mirror.
Scream them in the car.
Write them in your phone notes.
Make them your religion.

- *I am not responsible for someone else's inability to love me right.*
- *I will not confuse manipulation with passion ever again.*
- *I do not need closure. I need peace.*
- *I trust my gut. It never lied to me—I just didn't listen.*
- *I don't chase. I attract. What belongs to me respects me.*
- *I don't need to perform for love. I am already enough.*
- *I am not available for half-assed, emotionally unavailable bullshit.*
- *I am not what happened to me. I am what I choose next.*

BONUS WORTHY AF NEURO-HACK

Anchor your affirmations to a routine.

- *Say them while brushing your teeth.*
- *Say them while putting on moisturizer.*
- *Say them while lacing up your shoes.*

Why?

Because when your brain connects new beliefs to something automatic, those beliefs start becoming automatic, too. That's how we sneak the healing in. That's how we reprogram the pain.

Final Truth Bomb
Betrayal doesn't break you.
It shows you what was already fractured—so you can rebuild from truth, not illusion.

It's not your fault. But it is your responsibility to heal.

You don't get to rewrite what happened.
But you do get to write what happens next.

And it starts with two words:

I AM

Chapter 18: Burned By Love, Reborn In Truth

"Letting go wasn't weakness. It was the bravest thing I ever did"

This chapter is going to strip down the curated bullshit about grief—the flowers, the casseroles, the "they're in a better place" Hallmark-card garbage—and dive into the real shit no one warns you about:
- The rage.
- The guilt.
- The numbness.
- The weird relief you feel sometimes and then hate yourself for feeling.
- The kind of grief that makes brushing your damn teeth feel like a full-time job.

And we're not just talking about death. We're talking about all forms of loss: people, pets, breakups, miscarriages, divorces, the version of yourself you'll never be again. Because grief doesn't just show up in funerals—it shows up in flashbacks. It shows up in your fucking bones.

When Grief Shows Up Uninvited (and Doesn't Fucking Leave)

You know what no one tells you about grief?
It doesn't knock.
It doesn't ask permission.
It shows up like a drunk ex at 2 a.m.—sloppy, loud, and full of regret.
It crashes into your life, throws shit around, and somehow leaves you to clean up the mess. And just when you think it's over, guess who pops back up when you're at the damn grocery store holding a can of soup you didn't even want?

Grief.

It's a shapeshifter. One minute it's sadness. The next, it's rage. Then silence. Then full body sobbing in the shower while you're supposed to be getting ready for work.

And here's the kicker...

Grief doesn't always wait for death, sometimes we grieve:
- *The parent who never really showed up.*
- *The ex who's still alive but emotionally dead.*
- *The friend who ghosted you like you didn't bury secrets together.*
- *The baby you never got to hold.*
- *The version of yourself before the world broke your heart.*

Grief isn't just crying over a loss.
It's mourning what could've been.
What should've been.
What never fucking was.

Real Talk: Grief Is Not Linear

You've probably heard this lie, "Grief has 5 stages. You move through them, and then it's done.

Bullshit.

Grief has seasons.
Grief has triggers.
Grief has no respect for your plans or your calendar.

You don't just move through grief. You build a life around it, You build a life around the hole that's left. That hole might get smaller. You might get stronger. But some days, it still sucker-punches you. And that doesn't mean you're broken. It means you're human.

Truth Bomb: You're Not Weak Because You're Still Hurting

You're not pathetic because it's been "too long" and you're "still not over it, you're not crazy because you still have their number saved, you're not dramatic because you hear a certain song and completely lose your shit, you are grieving. And grief is love with nowhere to go.
But let me say this louder for the people in the back:
You are allowed to feel joy again.
You are allowed to fall in love again.
You are allowed to smile, laugh, move the fuck on—and still miss them.
That's not betrayal.
That's healing.

Personal Example: The Day I Forgot to Cry

There was a day, months into my grief, when I laughed so hard I actually snorted. And then, like clockwork, came the guilt.
"How dare you be happy?"
I felt like I was betraying the pain. Like if I wasn't suffering, I wasn't honouring the loss.
But that's the trap.
Grief wants to convince you that joy means forgetting.

But here's what I learned:

You don't have to choose. You can carry the love and still reclaim your life.

REALITY CHECK EXERCISE: Write the Goodbye You Never Got

1. Take a deep breath.
2. Write a letter to the person, the dream, the relationship you lost.
3. Say all the shit you never got to say. Uncensored. Raw. Angry. Ugly. Beautiful.
4. Then write this:

"I will always carry your memory, but I will know

When Grief and Guilt Go to Bed Together

You ever try to feel happy while grief is still breathing down your neck, it's like trying to dance with a 200-pound invisible backpack strapped to your chest. Every move forward feels heavy. Awkward. Like you're betraying something sacred just by existing without crying. That's what grief does and then guilt slides in like the toxic ex it is, whispering shit like:

- *"You should still be sad."*
- *"You're forgetting them."*
- *"You're moving on too fast."*
- *"How dare you enjoy anything?"*

Sound familiar?

Guilt is grief's nasty little twin—and it doesn't care if you've been suffering for weeks, months, or years. It just wants to keep you stuck. Because stuck feels safer than letting go. Safer than saying, "I still miss you… but I'm choosing to keep living anyway."

But here's the truth bomb that might piss some people off:

You don't owe your grief to anyone—not even the dead

You don't have to prove how much you loved someone by setting your own life on fire.

The Grief Loop: Where Your Past Keeps Replaying Itself

Ever notice how grief doesn't always feel fresh—but it still hits just as hard?

You can be years out and still:
- *Smell something and instantly fall apart.*
- *Hear a song and lose your breath.*
- *See their handwriting and suddenly forget how to function.*

Welcome to the Grief Loop.

It's not just a memory—it's a full-body experience. Your nervous system remembers what your mind has tried to forget.
You might be fine on the outside. You might have your lashes done, nails perfect, matching sweatsuit on point—but inside?
Your body's back in the trauma.
Back in the moment you lost them.
Back in the spiral of pain.
You think you're crazy.
You're not.
You're grieving.

Let's Get Real: What Grief Really Feels Like

It's not always sobbing into a pillow. Sometimes it's:
- *Rage at the wrong people.*
- *Avoiding places that used to bring joy.*
- *Numbness so deep you forget what joy feels like.*

- *Scrolling mindlessly at 2 a.m. because you're scared to sit with your own thoughts.*
- *Snapping at your kid because your bandwidth is fried.*

Grief doesn't just touch one part of you. It crawls into your relationships, your routines, your fucking identity and here's where it gets even more twisted, sometimes grief comes after the worst part is already over Like your body knew you had to hold it together until the chaos stopped—and then it broke.

Real-Life Example: The Betrayal Grief

There's a grief that hits when someone cheats on you. When you lose them not to death—but to disrespect.

That kind of grief is insidious. It's confusing. Because you don't get to mourn a good person—you mourn the person you thought they were. The future you planned. The love you gave. The faith you had in someone who wasn't worthy of it.

And then people say dumb shit like:
- *"Well at least he didn't die."*
- *"You can find someone new."*

No bitch. I don't want someone new.
I want my fucking peace back.

Grieving betrayal is brutal because the person who caused the pain is still breathing. Still posting. Still walking around like they didn't leave ashes behind.

Truth Bomb: You Can't Heal What You Pretend Doesn't Hurt

You can't bypass this part.
You can't manifestation-journal your way around grief.
You can't positive vibe your way past heartbreak.
You've got to sit in it.
Cry ugly.
Scream into a towel.
Talk to a wall if you need to.
Write the letter.
Burn the journal page.
Go full feral in the bathtub.

Let it out.

Because if you don't? That grief festers. It turns into resentment. Into self-hate. Into chronic pain and insomnia and lashing out at people who don't deserve it.

And baby, you've carried that weight long enough.

Mini-Exercise: The "Grief Guilt" Inventory
Grab a pen. Let's purge this shit.
Answer these three journal questions—no filter:
   1. *What do I feel guilty about when it comes to my grief?*
   2. *Who told me I had to stay sad to be respectful?*
   3. *What would healing actually look like if I stopped carrying everyone else's expectations?*
Then, write this:

"I am allowed to move forward.
I am allowed to remember and still rebuild.
Grief does not define me—my strength does."

The Little Things That Saved Me

Sometimes the thing that pulled me back wasn't big.
It wasn't therapy or an inspirational quote.
It was brushing my teeth.
Washing my hair.
Making a fucking sandwich.
Small things. Done anyway.
There were days when I'd stand in front of the mirror, puffy-faced and shattered, and whisper:
"You're still here. That's enough."

And it was.
longer carry the weight of your absence. I choose to keep living."

Your Breakthrough Starts Here

This is where we stop letting the past write the next chapter.
You've cried. You've cursed. You've cracked wide open.

Now? You fucking rise.

And no, I'm not here to hand you a Pinterest quote and send you on your way. I'm here to give you the real tools that helped me heal my shit, reclaim my power, and remember that I was never the problem—I was just the one who stayed too long in places I'd already outgrown.

THE WORTHY AF TRUTH

If you don't trust yourself, nothing else works.
Not your boundaries.
Not your intuition.
Not your healing.

Not even your new relationship.
Because you'll always be waiting for the other shoe to drop—and sweet girl, you'll be the one dropping it. That's what betrayal does.

But what heals that?
Let's break it down.

"I AM" STATEMENTS — YOUR DAILY REWIRE RITUAL

This shit changed my life. No exaggeration. You want a simple way to start building self-trust? This is it.

The Ritual:
Every morning—before you check your phone, open Instagram, or doomscroll your life away—you write 3 "I AM" statements.
Even if you don't believe them yet.
Even if they feel like lies at first.
You write them as if they're already true. Because you're reprogramming your brain, baby.
Real Examples:
- *I am trusting.*
- *I am trustworthy.*
- *I am safe with myself.*
- *I am beautiful.*
- *I am worthy of love.*
- *I am healing every damn day.*
- *I am a powerful woman who doesn't need permission to take up space.*

And when you run out of space in your journal?
Write them on your mirror, Say them while brushing your teeth.
Whisper them while you're pouring your coffee.

Speak them like you're casting a spell—because you are. Every time you say it, you're rewiring your brain. Every time you write it, you're building a new version of you.

JOURNAL PROMPTS TO HEAL GRIEF + BETRAYAL

These 7 prompts are about digging deep—into what hurt, what you lost, and what the fuck you're taking back.

Take your time. Go slow. These aren't cute little fluff prompts. They're truth serum.

1. What did betrayal take from me—and what am I reclaiming now?

2. What version of me did I lose in that relationship? Who am I Rebuilding Now?

3. What am I still blaming myself for that was never my fault?

4. If I believed I was truly worthy, how would I show up differently in my next relationship?

5. What red flags did I ignore—and what boundaries will I never break again for anyone?

6. What did I learn about myself through this heartbreak that I'm actually proud of?

_____
_____
_____
_____
_____
_____
_____
_____
_____
_____
_____
_____
_____
_____
_____
_____
_____
_____
_____
_____
_____
_____
_____

7. If I could speak to the version of me who stayed, what would I tell her now?

_____
_____
_____
_____
_____
_____
_____
_____
_____
_____
_____
_____
_____
_____
_____
_____
_____
_____
_____
_____
_____
_____
_____
_____
_____
_____

BREAKTHROUGH EXERCISE: THE TRUST REBUILD MAP

Let's get tactical.

This isn't about the other person. It's about you. This is how you begin to trust yourself again—not just in love, but in life.

STEP 1: Write out 3 times you knew your gut was right—and you ignored it.
Then write what happened because of that. No shame, just truth.

STEP 2: Now list 3 times you trusted yourself—and it worked out
These moments are evidence. Evidence that you can trust you. You've just been conditioned not to.

STEP 3: Choose 1 way to act on your intuition this week.
Even if it's small.
Especially if it's small.
You're building a muscle.

HEALING VISUALIZATION: CALLING YOURSELF BACK

You gave your energy to people who didn't deserve it. It's time to call it back.

Close your eyes. Breathe deep. Imagine every time you lost a piece of yourself—every fight, every moment you stayed too long, every time you silenced your voice.

Now visualize a glowing thread of light coming back to your body from each of those moments.

Feel your power return.
Feel yourself come home.

Say this out loud:

"I call back every part of me I gave away.
I forgive myself for forgetting who I was.
I am safe. I am whole. I am home."

Do this as often as you need.
Every time you feel empty—call yourself back.

REMEMBER THIS:

Betrayal was never about you.
Grief isn't a weakness.
And healing isn't linear—it's a fucking battlefield, and you're still standing.
You've got the scars.
Now build the Armour

AFFIRMATION

"I TRUST MYSELF, I FORGIVE MYSELF, I LOVE MYSELF AND NO ONE FERS TO TAKE MY WORTH AGAIN"

I Am Worthy AF

And no one gets to take my worth ever again."
"I trust myself.
I forgive myself.
I love myself.
And no one gets to take my worth ever again."

Chapter 19: Reclaiming Your Body, Food, And Fucking Sanity

"You're not a before and after photo-you're a whole damn story"

I used to think my body was the problem.
Too soft.
Too loud.
Too emotional.
Too much.
Too messy.
Too broken.
Too fucking "everything."

Every stretch mark? A reminder I wasn't good enough, every pound gained. A punishment, every time I bloated, broke out, felt pain, or didn't fit into the jeans I swore were my "goal jeans"? Proof. Proof that I had failed, That I was a failure, That I was somehow... less.

But that wasn't the truth.

That was shame, dressed up in cultural conditioning, family commentary, high school bullshit, and the kind of trauma that settles in your skin and whispers, "You're disgusting" every time you catch a glimpse of yourself naked in the mirror.

Let me be clear about something right now:

Your body is not a fucking apology.

And no — it never was.

TRAUMA STORED IN THE BODY IS REAL AS FUCK Let's talk science for a second, because this is more than just mindset fluff.

When you experience trauma — whether it's a breakup, emotional abuse, sexual assault, bullying, fat-shaming, medical gaslighting, or years of internalized unworthiness — it doesn't just float around in your brain like a sad thought bubble.

That shit gets stored.
In your nervous system.
In your gut.
In your muscles.
In your organs.
In the way your shoulders hunch when someone raises their voice.
In the way you flinch at compliments.
In the way your stomach drops when your partner says, "We need to talk."

This body you live in? She remembers everything.
And if we don't start talking to her with love, we'll keep repeating the shame cycle. Diet after diet. Punishment after punishment. Plastic surgery consults after bathroom breakdown.

But healing starts here.

I USED TO STARVE HER
Let's get honest.
I didn't treat my body like a temple. I treated her like a problem to fix. A curse to shrink. A battleground I fought on every damn day.
I over-exercised.
I under-ate.
I binged.
I punished.
I compared her to girls online who lived on green juice and Facetune.
I called her names I wouldn't even say to my worst enemy.

I was cruel.

And why? Because that's what I was taught.

That being pretty = worthy.
That being thin = lovable.
That being quiet = desirable.
That shrinking —
in body,
voice,
Opinion,
appetite,
Ambition — made me more acceptable.
And guess what, babe? **That's fucking false.**
That's the kind of generational trauma passed down like a family recipe for shame pie.

THE MOMENT, I KNEW IT HAD TO END

There was a day I caught myself calling my own body "disgusting" — out loud — in front of my daughter. She was watching me get dressed, and I muttered something like,
"Ugh, I look huge."
She was maybe 7 or 8. And she looked at me with wide eyes and said:
"But Mommy, you're not huge. You're perfect."

Cue the gut punch.

Right there, I realized I was teaching her what to think about her own body — and it scared the shit out of me. That was the moment I decided: This ends with me. I will not pass this shame down.

I will not raise another woman who thinks she has to earn her worth through her reflection.

So I started doing the work.

Not the kind of work that sells waist trainers or promotes detox teas.
The real work.

The body forgiveness.
The mirror rituals.
The nervous system healing.
The mornings I cried while telling myself I was beautiful because it felt like a lie… but I said it anyway.

Because I was done punishing myself.
Because I was done trying to earn worthiness in a world that profits from me believing I'm not enough.

YOUR BODY AFTER TRAUMA

If you've ever experienced:
- *Sexual trauma*
- *Medical trauma*
- *Body shaming from a parent, partner, or society*
- *Pregnancy loss*
- *Abortion*
- *Birth trauma*
- *Emotional neglect*
- *Or even just years of being ignored, dismissed, and unloved*

…then chances are, you don't feel safe in your body.
You may dissociate.

You may numb out.
You may fluctuate in weight, emotions, or energy levels.
You may struggle to be touched or need constant validation just to feel okay.

That's not "crazy." That's trauma physiology.
Your nervous system learned: "It's not safe to be here." So your body adapted by checking out, fighting back, or shutting down.

But the good news is: we can rewire that.

You can reclaim the relationship with your body, one breath, one touch, one "I love you anyway" at a time.

And I'll show you how.

This Body Is Worthy AF — Even When the World Said It Wasn't

Breaking the Mirror and Rewriting the Story
I used to avoid mirrors.

No joke.

I'd tilt them. Hang a towel over them. Angle the lighting just right. I wasn't trying to be mysterious—I was hiding from my own fucking reflection.

And when I did catch a glimpse of myself?

It wasn't "Oh hey, there's that badass, beautiful woman doing her best."

It was:

"Ugh. Look at your stomach."
"Jesus, your thighs."
"How did you let yourself get like this?"
"Pull it together—you look sloppy."

That voice? That wasn't mine.
That was my mom.
My high school boyfriend.
That bitchy cousin.
The magazines at the checkout line.
The doctor who told me to "just lose weight" when I came in for a thyroid issue.
The kid in 8th grade who mooed at me when I wore shorts.

I didn't create that voice….But I believed it.

And that's the worst part of body shame:

It doesn't need to scream to control you.
It just needs you to whisper it to yourself over and over again until it becomes truth.

THE BULLSHIT INHERITANCE: BODY SHAME IS PASSED DOWN

Let's call this what it is: inherited trauma.

We watched the women before us pinch their stomachs in the mirror.
Say "I'm being bad" when they ate a cookie.
Apologize for not being in full makeup at 9 a.m.
Talk about "getting their body back" after babies like it was a fucking loaner car.

And what did we learn?

That worth is tied to thinness.
That beauty means being invisible.
That having a body is something to apologize for.

And now here we are, adult women, still trying to undo the damage.

Still hoping some diet will give us the confidence the patriarchy stole.
Still thinking the answer to our loneliness is losing 10 pounds.
Still believing our stretch marks make us unworthy of love.

But what if we decided: It ends with me?

What if you stopped calling your body a "before photo"?
What if you treated her like a friend instead of a failed project?
What if we stopped talking shit about the very thing that's carried us through every trauma, breakup, death, birth, diagnosis, and fucking disappointment?

What if we just… stopped?

WHEN YOU'VE BEEN TO WAR WITH YOUR BODY

Let's talk about what it's like to live in a body you've hated for years.

It's like waking up every morning and going into battle—with yourself.
You check your stomach in the mirror.

You adjust your shirt to cover the part you hate.
You put on jeans and feel like a fraud.
You promise to "be good today."
You count your calories and your worth.
You scroll past gym influencers and feel shame just for eating.
You obsess. You restrict. You binge. You numb.
And the whole time, you're pretending like everything's fine.

Smile. Take the selfie. Post the quote But you're dying inside.

I remember sobbing in a dressing room once—because I didn't fit into the same size jeans I wore last year.
That's it.
That's all it took.
My whole day ruined. My worth plummeted. All because of a fucking number on a tag.

This is what body dysmorphia does.

It convinces you that your value is as flimsy as a waistband,
It makes you miss out on memories, sex, swimming, laughter, life.
Because you're too busy thinking, "What do I look like right now?"

Babe, you could be
feeling joy—but you're calculating angles.
You could be feeling love—but you're wondering if he notices your rolls.
You could be feeling free—but your shame has a death grip on your throat.

BODY RECLAMATION RITUALS (THAT ACTUALLY WORK)

You want to heal your body story?

You have to un-fuck your relationship with it. And here's how we start:

RITUAL ONE: THE "THANK YOU" SHOWER

This isn't a quick rinse and go. This is sacred.
You're going to take the most intentional, sensual, grateful-as-fuck shower of your life.
Instructions :
- *Strip completely. No shame. No judgments. Just you.*
- *As you lather your body, name what each part has done for you.*

  - *"Thank you legs, for carrying me through heartbreak."*
  - *"Thank you stomach, for holding me even when I hated you."*
  - *"Thank you arms, for hugging my child when I felt like breaking."*

-
- *Say it out loud.*
- *Cry if you need to. Laugh. Breathe. Let it be messy.*

Do this once a week. Watch how it changes your intimacy with your own skin.

RITUAL TWO: CLOTHES THAT FUCKING FIT

Stop saving clothes that don't fit like they used to.

You are not a failure because your body changed. You are a human.

Keeping a closet full of "goal jeans" is just hoarding emotional warfare.

Clean that shit out. Donate what makes you feel small. Buy what fits now. Not when you lose 15 lbs. Not when you tone up. Now.

You deserve to feel hot, comfortable, and confident TODAY.

RITUAL THREE: BOUNDARIES AROUND BODY TALK

If Aunt Carol can't stop commenting on your weight, your skin, your food choices—shut that shit down.

Script it if you have to:
- **"I'm not discussing my body right now."**
- **"That comment isn't helpful."**
- **"Let's talk about something else."**

Set the tone. Protect your peace. Reclaim your space.

WORTHY AF EXERCISES TO HEAL BODY SHAME

Each of these is designed to rewire the way you think, feel, and show up in your skin.

1. Write a letter from your body to you.
Let her tell you how it feels to be judged, hated, ignored. Then write back and tell her you're sorry—and ready to love her again.

2. List 10 things your body has done right.
Not how it looks. What it's done.

Examples:
- *"Kept breathing when I wanted to give up."*
- *"Birthed a baby."*
- *"Got me out of a toxic relationship."*
- *"Held space for my grief."*

3. Take 3 photos of yourself this week. Unposed. Unfiltered.
Post them if you're bold. Don't if you're not ready. But take them. Look at them. Say, "I'm still worthy as fuck."

4. Catch the Critic
Every time you think something shitty about your body this week, write it down. Then reframe it.
Critic: "Your thighs are huge."
Reframe: "These thighs are strong enough to stand back up."

5. Dance. Naked. With zero apologies.
Pick a song. Turn the lights On
Move your body. Feel your skin. Be there.
Not for him. Not for TikTok.
For you.
This is body liberation, bitch. Welcome to the revolution.

The Mirror Is a Mother fucker (But You're Stronger Than It)

Let's get one thing straight:
The mirror has lied to you.
It told you your stretch marks made you unlovable.
That your thighs needed a gap.
That your stomach should be flatter, tighter, smaller.

That your skin needed filters.
That your laugh lines were a problem instead of a celebration of joy.
The mirror doesn't show you the kindness in your heart,
The mirror doesn't reflect the fucking resilience you carry,
The mirror doesn't see how you stayed alive through trauma, heartbreak, postpartum, surgeries, and shame.
And yet… we let it decide our worth.

Fuck. That.

You want to know when my healing really started?
It wasn't the journaling.
It wasn't the therapy.
It wasn't even the morning "I am" statements.
It was the day I stood in front of the mirror—naked, raw, unfiltered—and didn't flinch.
That was the day I realized: I've been fighting the wrong enemy.
The enemy wasn't my thighs.
It was the belief that they made me less.
The enemy wasn't my skin texture.
It was the bullshit beauty standard that made me think I had to be pore-less to be powerful.
The enemy wasn't my body.
It was my shame.
And shame?
That bitch only survives when you're silent.

WHEN YOU START SHOWING UP LIKE YOU DESERVE TO BE SEEN

There's a shift that happens when you stop shrinking.
You walk differently. You take up space. You stop apologizing.
You post the fucking bikini picture.

You wear the dress.
You show up to the damn pool party.
You don't sit out of life anymore.
And people notice.
They say: "You're glowing."
But it's not a glow. It's freedom.
It's no longer asking for permission to exist.

Let's be real: it's not about the weight.
It's not about the cellulite.
It's about whether or not you believe you deserve joy, pleasure, confidence, now—not 20 pounds from now.

There is no finish line where your body finally earns the right to feel sexy.

You've been worthy all along.

LET'S TALK ABOUT SEX, BABY

Body shame doesn't just mess with your mirror. It messes with your mojo, You can't enjoy intimacy if you're in your own head the whole damn time.
If you're sucking in your stomach…
If you're mentally apologizing for your jiggle…
If you're afraid the lights will expose your flaws…
You're not present.
You're not connected.
You're not free.

I used to lay there wondering: Does he notice my cellulite, Meanwhile, I should've been thinking: Damn, I deserve this pleasure.
Because guess what? Worthy AF women don't fuck like they owe anyone anything.

We fuck like we own the damn room.

So if you need to dim the lights, do it.
If you need to leave your shirt on, cool.
But the goal?
Full-body acceptance that lets you be fully present in the moment.
Because sensuality isn't about size—it's about embodiment.

A NOTE FOR THE MOMS
You are not a before photo.
You are not a "bounce back" body.
You are not a woman who used to be hot.
You are a mother fucking miracle worker.

Whether you've birthed a baby, raised one, or healed yourself through generational trauma—

Your body has earned the right to be loved without condition.
Stop hiding behind your kids in photos.
Stop skipping the beach trip.
Stop declining invites because of how your arms look in sleeveless shirts.
Let your daughter see you
live,
love,
laugh,
and dance—in your actual skin.

Let your son know that women are beautiful when they're real, not retouched.

Let your inner child feel SAFE in the skin that once felt unsafe.

FINAL TOOLS TO BREAK THE CYCLE

You're not here just to read—you're here to heal.

So here's your final batch of Worthy AF Body Healing Tools for this chapter:

JOURNAL PROMPTS

1. What have I been taught to believe about my body that I no longer choose to believe?

2. What's one thing I've missed out on because of body shame?

_____
_____
_____
_____
_____
_____
_____
_____
_____
_____
_____
_____
_____
_____
_____
_____
_____
_____
_____
_____
_____
_____
_____
_____
_____
_____
_____

3. How has my body protected me—emotionally or physically?

4. What would I tell my 10-year-old self about beauty?

5. What does confidence feel like in my body—not look like, but feel like?

6. When do I feel most embodied, alive, or sexy?

7. What does it mean to me to be Worthy AF—exactly as I am today?

EXERCISES

1. Body Mirror Breakthrough
Stand in front of a mirror naked. Make eye contact. Say one kind thing. Then another. Do this for 7 days straight.

2. Clothing Audit
Go through your closet. Throw out every single item that makes you feel "not enough." Burn them if you're feeling spicy.

3. Worthy AF Photo Series
Pick a day. Get dolled up or don't. Take 5 photos that capture you as you are. No filters. Save them. Frame one.

4. Eat the Fucking Cake
Whatever your food "shame" item is—pizza, pasta, cake—eat it with zero guilt. Enjoy every damn bite. Your worth isn't calorie-dependent.

5. The Body Love Playlist
Create a playlist that makes you feel sexy, alive, strong. Dance to it. Weekly. Naked. Yes, again.

FINAL WORDS (AND A TRUTH BOMB)

Your body isn't broken.
It isn't behind.
It isn't a project.
It's a goddamn miracle.

Every roll. Every stretch mark. Every scar. Every curve. Every inch.

You are worthy as fuck in this body.

Not ten pounds from now. Not after the detox. Not in next season's jeans.

Now.

And if anyone tells you otherwise—tell them to read this fucking book.*

Because your body isn't up for debate.
And your worth isn't up for negotiation.

Affirmation
I am worthy as fuck—in this body, in this moment, no matter what the mirror says.

I am worthy as fuck

CHAPTER 20: Boundary Breakdowns & the Bullshit We Swallow

"If love requires self-abandonment, it's not love. It's emotional blackmail"

The Slow Death of Self-Respect

Let's call it what it is: every time you said "yes" when your gut screamed "fuck no," you weren't being kind—you were betraying yourself.

Let's sit with that for a second.

We glamorize boundaries on Pinterest like they're these cute little affirmations:
"I'm protecting my peace."
"I'm prioritizing my energy."
Blah. Blah. Blah.

But real boundaries?
They're gritty.
They're uncomfortable.
They piss people off.
Because real boundaries aren't just fences—they're firewalls. They're the moments you say, "No, I'm not available for that," even if it makes you look like the villain. They're the nights you turn down a man who's bad for you—not because you don't want to see him, but because you know seeing him will cost you a piece of your self-worth you've worked too fucking hard to rebuild.

This chapter is about the cost of constantly breaking your own boundaries.
Because let me tell you—when you don't respect your limits, you end up swallowing shit you were never meant to digest.

And eventually, it shows up in your body.
In your bloating.

Your inflammation.
Your exhaustion.
Your addiction to caffeine and chaos and carbs and needing someone—anyone—to validate your existence.

Boundary breakdowns aren't always loud.
Sometimes they look like:
- *"I'll just stay quiet to avoid the fight."*
- *"It's fine, I'll do it myself."*
- *"They didn't mean it like that."*
- *"I'll start fresh Monday."*

Sound familiar?

We don't even notice the ways we're self-abandoning because we've normalized it.
It becomes second nature. Especially if you grew up being the fixer. The peacekeeper. The overachiever.
If you were parentified as a child—if you had to be the emotional support person for your caregivers, or if your needs were always last—then guess what? Boundaries feel unsafe to you.
You learned that love is earned.
That peace is your responsibility.
That saying "no" equals rejection or punishment.
So now?
You keep people around who treat you like shit because your nervous system is wired for chaos.
You self-soothe with sugar, scrolling, sex, and substances because you don't know how to sit with your own discomfort.
You don't know how to choose yourself without guilt.
So you keep choosing people, patterns, and pain that reinforce the belief:
I'm not worthy unless I'm useful.

Let me tell you something that might sting—but you need to hear it:
Being needed isn't the same as being loved.
And being the "strong one" doesn't make you invincible—it makes you invisible.
You disappear under the weight of everyone else's expectations. You carry their guilt, their shame, their fuckups.
And then you wonder why you feel so fucking tired all the time.

Because sis, you are operating from emotional bankruptcy.

You Can't Heal While You're Still People-Pleasing

Let's get one thing straight: you can't heal while you're still people-pleasing.
You can't find peace if you're addicted to being liked.
And you sure as hell can't love yourself if every time you feel uncomfortable, you run back to the very thing that's breaking you.

Let me say that louder for the self-abandoners in the back:
You will never find safety in people who require you to betray yourself to be loved.

But that's what we've been doing, right?
Putting ourselves on sale.
Shrinking to fit.
Saying "yes" when we want to scream "fuck no."
Making ourselves small so someone else can feel big.
And then we wonder why we feel resentful.
Why we lash out over "small things."

Why we binge eat or binge text or binge drink the second someone ignores us, ghosts us, or disrespects us.

That's not you being "too emotional."

That's your nervous system screaming, "I'm done being ignored."

You didn't get addicted to the food or the drink or the drama—you got addicted to the temporary relief it gave you from the pain of self-abandonment.

Let that one settle in your gut.

Because healing doesn't start when you light a fucking candle and journal about your ex.

It starts when you look in the mirror and say:

"I'm the reason I keep getting hurt—because I keep putting myself in situations that hurt me. And I'm done."

That's the line in the sand.
That's the moment the game changes.

Let's talk about boundaries and addiction.

People love to think of addiction as a chemical dependency. Booze. Pills. Weed. Cocaine.

But let me hit you with this truth bomb:

Addiction is anything you use to escape yourself.

So, when you're scrolling TikTok for four hours because you don't want to feel lonely?
That's addiction.

When you text your ex just to feel wanted—even when you know he's toxic as hell?
That's addiction.

When you keep yourself so busy you don't have a single fucking minute to sit with your own thoughts?
Yup. **That's addiction.**

And it all stems from the same root: you don't feel safe inside yourself.

You don't trust that your feelings are valid.
You don't believe your needs matter.
You don't even know who the hell you are without being in "fix-it" mode for someone else.

So you numb it.

And here's the sneaky part: it doesn't look like **addiction.**
It looks like being "nice."
Like being "the strong one."
Like being a good friend, a good partner, a good mom.

But if you're constantly crossing your own boundaries to be those things?
If you're betraying yourself daily just to keep the peace?

That's not love. That's martyrdom.
And martyrdom is the most toxic addiction of all.

Breakthrough Exercise:
Grab your journal and write this question at the top:
"What pain Am I still trying to avoid by breaking my own boundaries?"
Don't filter it. Don't try to be poetic. Be raw. Be real. Let it pour out. The truth is in there—you've just been silencing it to keep others comfortable.

Now list five boundaries you've broken recently. Be specific.
Then beside each one, write what it cost you emotionally, physically, mentally.

Example:

- *Said yes to babysitting when I was exhausted → Result: resentment, skipped workout, stress binge*
- *Answered my ex's call at 11 p.m. → Result: anxiety spike, self-judgment, poor sleep*

Once you're done, write this at the bottom of the page:

"I am done betraying myself to be digestible for others."

Say it out loud. Like you mean it. Because your nervous system needs to hear it from you.

Rebuilding Boundaries & Reclaiming Your Power

So now you've hit the wall. You've seen where your broken boundaries have left you bleeding. You've faced the truth that numbing your pain only delays your healing. You've written the receipts.

But now what?

This is where most people get stuck.
They say things like:
- *"I've just never been good at saying no."*
- *"I don't want to seem selfish."*
- *"I hate confrontation."*
- *"They'll be mad at me."*

And my personal favourite:
"It's just easier to do it myself."

Easier?
EASIER?!

Girl,
Easier is what got you exhausted.
Easier is what made you carry the mental load of three people while still apologizing for not doing enough.
Easier is how you ended up crying on the bathroom floor with no one checking on you because you trained everyone around you to believe that you're fine even when you're fucking dying inside.

Let's kill the myth once and for all:

Boundaries are not mean. Boundaries are not selfish. Boundaries are self-respect. Period.

And if your boundary makes someone uncomfortable?

That's their emotional immaturity, not your problem to fix.

You're not here to babysit grown ass adults through your healing.

Let's break this all the way down.

Boundary: "No."
That's it. That's the whole sentence.
Not "No, but maybe another time."
Not "No, I'm so sorry, I wish I could."
Just: No.

Boundary: "I don't engage in disrespectful conversations."
When someone starts yelling, gaslighting, or manipulating—shut it down. You don't owe anyone your peace.

Boundary: "I don't explain myself to people committed to misunderstanding me."
We spend too much time trying to "prove" our worth to people who don't deserve a front row seat to our lives. Revoke their ticket.

Boundary: "If it costs me my peace, it's too expensive."
Relationships, jobs, friendships—if you're constantly anxious, walking on eggshells, or second-guessing yourself, that's not love. That's emotional bankruptcy.

Self-Soothing vs. Self-Respect

Let's talk about that wine glass in your hand.
That box of cookies.

That situationship you keep revisiting like it's a fucking Netflix show.
That's self-soothing.
It's what we do when we're trying to regulate pain without addressing it.
But here's the truth: you can't self-soothe your way out of self-betrayal.

The only way to stop feeling like shit about yourself is to stop doing things that make you feel like shit.
Radical, I know.

And look—I'm not saying you need to become some Zen monk who never snaps or spirals.
I'm saying you need to make a commitment to yourself:

"I will stop choosing temporary comfort over permanent peace."

Journal Prompts & Exercises:

1. What does self-respect look like for you? Describe it. Get specific. Does it mean getting more sleep? Not answering texts past a certain hour? Saying no to people who drain you?

_____
_____
_____
_____
_____
_____
_____
_____
_____
_____
_____
_____
_____
_____
_____
_____
_____
_____
_____
_____
_____
_____
_____
_____

2. Where have you replaced boundaries with bandaids?

_____
_____
_____
_____
_____
_____
_____
_____
_____
_____
_____
_____
_____
_____
_____
_____
_____
_____
_____
_____
_____
_____
_____
_____
_____
_____
_____
_____

3. What areas of your life have you been patching with temporary solutions instead of creating lasting change?

4. What's one boundary you're afraid to set? Write it out. Then write why it scares you. Then write what might change if you set it anyway.

5. List five self-soothing behaviours you turn to when you feel unworthy.
For each one, write the emotion you're trying to escape. This gives you clarity—and clarity is power.

6. **Create a Boundary Comeback Plan.**
Choose one relationship or situation in your life where you feel drained. Write:
- The boundary you need
- The script you'll use to set it (short, clear, firm)
- The action you'll take if it's not respected

_____
_____
_____
_____
_____
_____
_____
_____
_____
_____
_____
_____
_____
_____
_____
_____
_____
_____
_____
_____
_____
_____
_____
_____
_____
_____

7. Where in my life am I calling "love", "loyalty" or "being a good person" - when really I'm just abandoning myself?

Closing Reminder

You're not broken because you over-gave.
You're not weak because you self-soothed.
You were just surviving.

But baby—you're not here to survive. You're here to THRIVE.

And thriving starts with this:

"I don't shrink anymore. I don't chase. I don't explain. I don't bend.
I know who the fuck I am, and I act like it."

Daily "I Am" Statements (Advanced Level Edition):
- *I am the boundary.*
- *I am the storm and the shelter.*
- *I am the calm that doesn't need chaos to feel alive.*
- *I am the voice that says "enough" and means it.*
- *I am no longer abandoning myself for love I have to earn.*
- *I am worthy without permission.*
- *I am a healed woman, not a hollow one.*
-

I AM WORTHY AS FUCK

Chapter 21: Comparison Is A Thieving Little Bitch

"She's not prettier, smarter, or. more successful- you're just scrolling through her highlight reel while choking on your own self-doubt"

You ever scroll Instagram at 10 PM in your oversized hoodie, surrounded by laundry, hair in a bun that's holding on for dear life, and suddenly you're spiralling because some bitch named Chloe is sipping a green smoothie on a yacht with abs so tight they could slice prosciutto?

Yeah. Welcome to the comparison hangover.
And spoiler alert: it's a hell of a drug.

This chapter is about healing the kind of trauma that doesn't always come from one big explosion—it comes from a thousand tiny cuts.
Every influencer post.
Every "clean girl aesthetic."
Every perfectly filtered wedding video while you're heating up chicken nuggets for one.

And we convince ourselves that they've figured it out, and we… clearly have not.

But here's the truth bomb:

Comparison is the thief of self-worth, and in this digital age, that motherfucker is robbing women blind.

So let's talk about the damage it's done, how to detox from it, and what it really takes to feel worthy in a world that profits from your insecurity.

The "Should" Show

It starts innocently.

"I should work out more."
"I should eat cleaner."
"I should be further ahead by now."
"I should be married. I should have kids. I should be making six figures. I should have clear skin and a skincare fridge."

And suddenly, your entire life is a highlight reel of what you're not.

Let's be clear: you are not behind.
You're just not on a bullshit timeline designed by strangers trying to sell you collagen.

What people call "motivation" online is often just curated shame.
It's why you feel like shit after a scroll session.
It's why you start thinking that if you just bought the right leggings or got the right morning routine, your life would magically fix itself.

But baby, healing doesn't come from a Stanley cup and an aesthetic planner.
It comes from the moment you say, "I'm done outsourcing my worth to the internet."

How Comparison Screws with Your Nervous System

Let's get scientific for a second.
Every time you compare yourself to someone else, your brain lights up the same stress pathways that get triggered when you're in danger.

That's right.

Your brain literally thinks you're being attacked—and your nervous system responds with cortisol, anxiety, and shame.

Now imagine doing that 10, 20, 30 times a day.
Welcome to modern womanhood.

Here's the catch: your nervous system isn't broken. It's doing its job.
What's broken is the belief that your value is determined by your productivity, your body, your likes, or your relationship status.

You can't hate yourself into healing.
You can't scroll your way into self-worth.
You have to reclaim your identity.
And that means setting boundaries with what you consume.

Reality Check Time (Buckle Up)
Let's break this myth of the "put together" woman.
- *The woman with the designer bag? Might be in debt.*
- *The girl with the six-pack? Might hate her body.*
- *The couple posting daily "relationship goals" reels? Might be sleeping in separate beds.*
- *The girl you envy on TikTok for being so confident? Might be re-filming that video for the 27th time and crying between takes.*

No one posts their breakdowns. They post their brand.

And half the time, that brand is bullshit.

Comparison is like looking in a funhouse mirror—you see a distorted version of reality and assume you're the problem. But you're not.

The problem is this warped culture that says:

- *You must hustle 24/7.*
- *You must be effortlessly pretty.*
- *You must heal your trauma and post about it… but don't be too messy.*

Fuck. That.

You don't owe the world a polished version of your healing. You owe yourself honesty, grace, and the commitment to your own damn path.

The Detox Starts Here

Let's get tactical.
If you're gonna heal from comparison trauma, you need a digital and emotional detox:

1. Unfollow the Trigger Queens.
If someone makes you feel like shit—even unintentionally—it's okay to mute, unfollow, or block. Your mental health isn't up for debate.

2. Clean Up Your Feed.
Follow people who inspire you without making you feel inadequate. People who are real. Messy. Honest. People who make you exhale instead of spiral.

3. Schedule Comparison Breaks.
Limit your scroll time. Literally set a timer. If you wouldn't invite someone to live rent-free in your head IRL, don't let them do it online.

4. Practice Mirror Moments.
Once a day, look yourself in the eyes and say three "I Am" statements—loud and proud.

No whispering. No eye rolls. Own that shit.

I Am Statements for Comparison Recovery
- *I am enough, even when I don't feel like it.*
- *I am more than my likes, comments, or weight.*
- *I am worthy of love without a filter.*
- *I am not for everyone—and that's a superpower.*
- *I am healing at my own pace, and that's okay.*
- *I am whole, right now, not "someday."*

The Cost of "Not Enough" and the Cure You Didn't Know You Needed

Let me ask you something:
How much of your anxiety is coming from the pressure to be someone you're not?
Seriously.
How many times have you said:
- "Once I lose the weight, I'll be happier."
- "If I just post more, maybe I'll finally go viral."
- "When I get my shit together, I'll finally feel worthy."

But the problem isn't your weight, your content strategy, or your planner.
The problem is chronic worthlessness disguised as ambition.

Comparison doesn't motivate.
It suffocates.

And we've normalized that suffocation. We wear it like a fucking badge of honour.
We call it "being realistic."
We call it "striving for more."
But really?

It's self-abandonment in a cute little productivity outfit.

Let me remind you of something real quick:
Just because someone else is winning doesn't mean you're losing.
Your life is not behind.
Your body is not wrong.
Your journey is not late.
It's just not theirs.
And that's not only okay—it's fucking magic.

The Silent Self-Worth Sabotage

Let's talk about something people don't want to admit: Sometimes, comparison becomes your identity.
You don't know who you are without the struggle of trying to be better.

You spend so much time chasing your next glow-up that you've forgotten how to be proud of where you are right now.

You keep thinking that being "better" will finally earn you the love, attention, or validation you were denied as a kid—or in that relationship—or by that job that made you feel disposable.

And that's the sneaky part.

Comparison isn't just about jealousy. It's about grief.
It's grieving the version of you who was never fully seen.
And instead of sitting with that grief, you mask it with hustle, filters, and self-criticism.

But hear this:

You are not a problem to fix. You are a person to love.

Real Talk from the Mirror

Let me take you back to a Tuesday morning that cracked me open.

I had just gotten off a scroll binge—some girl I used to know posted her new house, perfect husband, and fucking beige baby nursery with the matching crib, wallpaper, and decorative "BABY LOVE" sign above it like a damn Pinterest shrine.

And here I was—single, surviving, eating a protein bar in my car, questioning every life choice I'd ever made.

I remember slamming my mirror shut and thinking, "What the fuck am I even doing?"

And that voice came in hot:

"If you were prettier, if you worked harder, if you had it together…"

But I stopped.
I stopped because I realized that voice didn't even belong to me.

That voice was a collection of every magazine cover I'd ever read.
Every mean girl comment I internalized.

Every man who made me feel replaceable.
Every moment society whispered,
"Be more.
* Be less.*
* Be better."*

And I said, "Not today."

That morning, I wrote on my bathroom mirror:
"I'm not chasing her life. I'm building mine."
And that became a ritual.
Every day, I added another sticky note. Another "I Am." Not because I believed them right away—but because I wanted to.

The Exercise That Changed Everything

Here's your mirror ritual:

Step 1: Get a dry erase marker or post-it notes.
Step 2: Write 3 "I Am" statements every morning before checking your phone.
Step 3: Say them OUT LOUD. Not in your head. Not in a whisper. OWN IT.

Examples:
- *I am not behind.*
- *I am not too much.*
- *I am allowed to take up space.*
- *I am whole even when healing.*
- *I am building a life I'm proud of—even if it's messy.*

And yes, at first, it will feel ridiculous. Cringe, even. But one day, you'll say them and believe it.
And that moment? That's when comparison loses.

Why This Healing Is Bigger Than You

This shit isn't just about your confidence.
It's generational.

When we heal our worthiness wounds, we stop the cycle.
We show our kids—our friends—our inner child—that we don't have to earn love by being perfect.
We just have to be real.

You're not just doing this for you.
You're doing this for every version of you that ever felt like a shadow in someone else's spotlight.

You're doing it for the girl who never thought she was pretty enough, smart enough, thin enough, cool enough, soft enough.

You're doing it for the woman who finally said:
"I'm enough. I've always been enough. And I don't need the fucking algorithm to confirm it."

Journal Prompts: Burn the Comparison

1. What version of "her" do you compare yourself to the most—and what does she represent?

2. When did you first learn that your worth was tied to performance, appearance, or approval?

3. Who would you be if you stopped trying to "catch up" to someone else's life?

4. Write a letter to the younger you who didn't know her worth. What does she need to hear?

5. What social media boundaries do you need to put in place to protect your peace?

6. What are 5 things you've accomplished that you've never given yourself credit for?

7. If you believed you were already enough, how would your daily life look different?

The Worthy AF Healing Mantra

"I am not a copy. I am the fucking original.
I am worthy, even when it's quiet.
I don't need to chase her life—I am building mine.
And every damn day, I show up like I believe that."

I AM WORTHY AS FUCK

CHAPTER 22: Silent as a MOTHERfucker – The Guilt No One Talks About

"Mom guilt is the prison you build with other people's expectations- then sentence yourself to life without fucking parole"

You know what no one warns you about? That once you become a mom, you also become a walking, talking guilt magnet. Like a human sponge for shame. From the second that pee stick shows two lines, it's like society opens a tab under your name titled: "Shit She'll Blame Herself for Forever."

And trust me, that tab never closes.

You'll feel guilty
For what you eat while pregnant.
For what kind of birth you have.
For how long you breastfeed—or if you don't.
For going back to work.
For staying home.
For yelling.
For being too soft.
For the screen time.
For the lack of screen time.
For literally everything.

It's like guilt is the seasoning in the motherhood stew. And the worst part?

We're so conditioned to it that we don't even talk about it. Not to our friends. Not to our partners. Not even to ourselves.

We just carry it.
In the bags under our eyes.
In the tone we use with ourselves when we make a mistake.
In the way we second-guess every decision.
In the way we cry in the shower when no one's looking.

It's silent.

It's suffocating.
And it's fucking exhausting.

But here's the part no one dares to say out loud:
the guilt we carry isn't always about our kids. A lot of it? It's about us. It's about who we used to be. It's about grieving the woman we were before the world told us we had to be perfect to be good enough.

Because somewhere along the line, we bought the lie that good moms don't mess up.
That good moms don't cry in their cars.
That good moms don't feel like running away.
That good moms always get it right.

Bull. Shit.

I've met a lot of moms in my life. And you know what the strongest ones have in common?
They've all had a moment where they looked in the mirror and whispered, "I'm failing."
Even when they weren't.
Even when they were fucking killing it.

Because mom guilt doesn't need logic to thrive.
It just needs silence.
It needs shame.
It needs us to suffer quietly so it can grow roots in our bones.

And this chapter? This chapter is your eviction notice.

Because we're not doing this anymore.

We're not pretending that mom guilt is some badge of honour.
We're not accepting that self-sacrifice is the price of love.
We're not raising the next generation from a place of burnout and buried resentment.
We're healing.
We're talking about it.
We're calling that shit out.

Because the truth is—if you don't heal your guilt, it will bleed into your parenting.

It'll show up in how quickly you snap when your kid spills juice.
It'll show up when you avoid setting boundaries because you're afraid to be the "mean mom."
It'll show up in your nervous system, in your health, in your body.
And worst of all? It'll show up in your child's inner voice.

And I don't know about you, but I refuse to pass this shit down.

When You're Everything… and It Still Feels Like Not Enough

You send your kid to their dad's every weekend?
Cue the side-eyes.

"Oh… must be hard for them not to have their mom."

Really? Because I thought it was fucking hard being the only parent doing it all five days a week—juggling work, bills, appointments, meltdowns, and trying to make sure my kid eats something green that isn't a gummy bear.

But no—clearly, I'm the monster here for needing two goddamn days to breathe and maybe do laundry in peace.

Let's be clear: kids need **BOTH** parents.

If the father is showing up, being safe, supportive, and present—why the hell are we still pushing this "mom has to be everything" bullshit? We don't shame dads for taking breaks or going golfing or hitting the gym. But when a mom does it?

The guilt eats us alive.

And don't even get me started on daycare guilt.
The number of mornings I dropped my kid off with a painted-on smile, then sobbed in the car because someone once made a comment like,
"I could never let someone else raise my child."

Well, Karen, some of us don't have the luxury of a husband with a six-figure salary and 3:30pm yoga.
Some of us have to fucking hustle.
And while we're hustling? We carry this loop in our head:
"Are they okay?"
"Did I hug them enough this morning?"
"Did I snap too hard about the socks on the floor?"
"Did they feel loved, or just rushed?"
"Will they grow up resenting me?"

No one told us motherhood came with a full-time mental courtroom in our heads.

But here we are—judge, jury, and executioner—all against ourselves.

Now let's get raw about something else:

The mom guilt of dating.

Holy hell. Where do I start?

The moment you start talking to someone new, the pressure sets in:
Do I introduce them?
How long do I wait?
What if it doesn't work? Am I fucking up my kid?

You're not just navigating your own heart anymore—you're carrying theirs too. Every heartbreak, every breakup, every "what happened to so-and-so?" hits different when your kid gets attached.

So we self-sabotage.
We ghost people before it gets serious.
We convince ourselves we're better off alone.
Because dating while mothering is like walking a tightrope—with judgment on one side and shame on the other.

And even when we do find someone who seems decent, the world loves to whisper:
"Shouldn't you be focusing on your child right now?"

As if having a personal life somehow makes you a shittier mom.

Let me make this crystal fucking clear:

You are allowed to have love.
You are allowed to have joy.
You are allowed to want sex, affection, companionship, fun, peace—whatever the fuck you want—AND be a good mother.

You being whole doesn't take a damn thing away from your child. In fact, it shows them what thriving looks like.

But try telling that to the voice in your head when you're out for drinks with your friends and you see a post about someone doing "mom and me" crafts. And suddenly you're thinking:

Should I be home right now? Am I being selfish? Is she going to remember I missed bedtime?

That voice is a lying little bitch.

Because what your kid remembers isn't always the bedtime—they remember who you were at the end of the day. Were you resentful? Exhausted? Snapping at every question? Or were you occasionally recharged, smiling, dancing in the kitchen, and emotionally present because you took a fucking break?

Mom guilt doesn't come from motherhood—it comes from a society that expects women to be self-sacrificing martyrs.

And God forbid you raise your voice.
Or set a boundary.
Or say, "I need time for me."
Suddenly you're
"too emotional,"
"too hard,"
"not soft enough."

But if you bend over backwards, they call you "too much" anyway.

So here's the truth bomb:

You will never be perfect.
You will fuck up.
You will miss things.
You will cry in your car.
You will do your best and still question yourself.

And still...
You're a good mom.

You're a great fucking mom.
Not because you never make mistakes.
But because you keep showing up—with love, with effort, and with guilt that you shouldn't even have to carry.

The Undoing of Guilt, The Becoming of Worthy AF

Let's get brutally honest.

Mom guilt isn't just a feeling—it's a fucking identity crisis.
It's waking up at 3 a.m. wondering if that tantrum your kid had was because you didn't play enough that day... or because they secretly hate you.
It's feeling like every meltdown, every struggle, every hiccup in their life is somehow your fault.
And it's never-ending.

But here's the wild thing no one tells you:

Guilt is often the mask for powerlessness.
When we feel like we can't fix everything for our kids, we try to compensate with guilt.
Because guilt feels like we're doing something.
We beat ourselves up as a form of self-punishment, thinking maybe that's what a "good mom" does. Maybe this is the price we pay for every missed school play or takeout dinner.

No. Fuck that noise.

Let me say it louder for the perfectionist martyrs in the back:

Guilt does not make you a better mother. Presence does. Sacrificing your entire identity does not make you more loving. Showing your child what self-respect looks like does.

Let's rewrite what motherhood actually means.

You went through trauma and chose to heal?
You didn't hand that pain to your kid like a fucked-up generational baton?
You showed them what it looks like to rise from the ashes, not stay buried in them?
That's not failure.
That's not selfish.
That's not weak.

That's a fucking superpower.

When my daughter watched me rebuild my life, I didn't say a word—
but she saw everything.
She saw the tears I tried to hide.

She saw the way I duct-taped my dignity together after heartbreak.
She saw me exhausted, angry, still getting sh*t done.

But most of all? She saw me evolve.

She saw me change.

And over time, she started saying things like:
"Mom, you look happier."
"You don't get mad the same anymore."
"I like when you smile like that."

That's when it hit me.

My glow-up wasn't just for me. It was for her.
And it happened in front of her—not in spite of her.

Because I stopped trying to be the mom with the Pinterest-perfect lunchboxes and started being the mom who shows up real, messy, imperfect, and present.

That's how you shatter generational cycles.
That's how you raise daughters who don't have to spend their 30s in therapy trying to unpack why they never felt enough.

So if you've ever laid in bed wondering:
- *Did I fuck this up too much already?*
- *Am I ruining them?*
- *Will they remember the yelling? The silence? The days I couldn't even look at myself in the mirror.*

Here's the truth.

They will remember…
But they will also remember how you owned your shit.
How you apologized.
How you grew.
How you kept choosing to be better.

And yes, maybe you lost your shit sometimes.
Maybe you cried in the pantry or screamed into a pillow or forgot picture day again.
But guess what?
You also fed them.
And hugged them.
And held them when the world felt scary.
And you never gave up on yourself—even when you wanted to.

And that?
That's mothering.
That's the whole damn point.

So, let's stop pretending mom guilt is something noble.
It's not.
It's a fucking energy leak.
And your kids don't want a martyr—they want a mother who knows her worth and models what that looks like.

So, here's how we release the guilt—because awareness alone doesn't cut it. You need a ritual. A practice. A daily middle finger to the guilt that's tried to own you.
MOM GUILT RELEASE RITUAL:

Step 1: The Mirror Talk

Write these "I Am" statements with a Sharpie on your bathroom mirror (yes, I'm serious):
- *I am doing enough.*
- *I am allowed to be happy.*
- *I am a good mom even when I need a break.*
- *I am showing my child what strength looks like.*
  Say them every morning until you believe them—or fake it until the truth kicks in.

Step 2: Write the Lies Down
Every time guilt creeps in, write the thought. Then under it, write the actual truth.
Example:
"I'm a bad mom for working late."
→ " I'm providing for my family and showing them what ambition looks like."

Step 3: Mom Guilt Burn List
Write down everything you're holding shame around. Dating. Takeout. Divorce. Missing one fucking soccer game.
Burn it.
Safely. In a fireproof dish. With intention.
Say this:
"I release the guilt. I claim my wholeness. I mother from truth, not shame."

Step 4: Build Your Worthy AF Legacy
Start a list called "Shit I've Done Right."
Don't stop at 5. Aim for 50.
Keep it in your phone. Look at it when guilt hits.
Because YOU are the fucking magic. Not the guilt.

Journal Prompts for Breaking the Guilt Loop:

1. What is one area I'm hardest on myself as a mom? Where did that belief come from?

2. What do I want my child to believe about motherhood when they grow up?

3. What moments have made me feel like a failure... and what would I say to a friend who told me the same story?

4. How do I define being a "good mom"? Is that definition even mine?

_____
_____
_____
_____
_____
_____
_____
_____
_____
_____
_____
_____
_____
_____
_____
_____
_____
_____
_____
_____
_____
_____
_____
_____
_____
_____
_____
_____

5. What's one thing I can let go of today that doesn't actually make me a better parent?

_____
_____
_____
_____
_____
_____
_____
_____
_____
_____
_____
_____
_____
_____
_____
_____
_____
_____
_____
_____
_____
_____
_____
_____
_____
_____
_____
_____
_____

6. How has my child benefited from seeing me grow, not just hold it together?

7. What message do I want my child to internalize every time they watch me take care of myself?

Final Word:

If you've made it this far, I need you to hear me.

You are not a fuck-up.
You are not too late.
You are not a bad mom because you needed time, space, love, or a damn glass of wine and two hours of Netflix in silence.

You are not selfish for healing.
You're brave as fuck.

Your guilt doesn't get the final say.
Your growth does.

And your kids?

They're not looking for perfect.
They're looking for you.

The real, flawed, worthy as fuck version—who knows the power of getting back up and saying:

I AM WORTHY AF

FINAL GOODBYE: One Last Fuck You To Who You Use To Be

"You don't Owe anyone an explanation or an apology for becoming a BADASS"

To the woman holding this book like it just saved her life—

I want you to pause.
Take a deep breath.
And feel what you've just done.

You didn't just read a book.
You faced your demons.
You unpacked your childhood.
You ripped the bandaid off betrayal.
You sat with the grief.
You chose to meet your pain with truth instead of denial.

You didn't skip the ugly parts.
You didn't spiritual bypass your trauma with cute mantras or detox teas.
You didn't make it prettier than it was.

You walked through hell in high heels and came out holding your fucking crown.

This book was never meant to fix you. Because you were never broken.
You were buried—under expectations, shame, trauma, abuse, society, your own self-doubt—and you just clawed your way back to the surface.

Now that you're here, I want you to remember this:

You will never be the same again.

You are not "going back" to who you were before him, or before the pain, or before the world told you that you had to be quiet, small, pretty, agreeable, healed, or "easy to love."

That version of you doesn't exist anymore.
And thank fucking god for that.

You're not soft anymore—you're sovereign.
You're not looking for approval—you've found your power.
You're not waiting for someone to choose you—you've chosen yourself.

And if anyone dares to ask what changed?

You look them dead in the eye and say:

"I remembered who the fuck I am."

From here on out, you live like it.

You wear what the fuck you want.
You speak up without apologizing.
You walk away from anything that makes your nervous system scream.
You hold your boundaries like a goddess guarding gold.
You stop begging for crumbs and start demanding feasts.
You mother your damn self the way you always needed.

And when the guilt creeps in?
When the shame whispers that you're "too much" or "not enough"?

You light a match.
And you burn that shit down.

You don't owe this world your silence, your suffering, or your smallness.

You owe it your aliveness.

So go live.
Go speak.
Go create, love, break, rebuild, and rise again.

Go become the woman this world has never seen before.

You are Worthy as Fuck.
And now? You fucking know it.

With love, fire, and full-body chills,
-Brandee 🖤

THE FINAL AFFIRMATION
(Read this out loud like you fucking mean it.)

I am not healing to be palatable.
I am not rising to be relatable.
I am the storm they warned you about—
and the bitch who owns the thunder.

I'm not a survivor.
I'm a fucking weapon.
Sharpened by betrayal.
Polished by pain.
And aimed at everything they said I'd never become.

I no longer water myself down for fragile egos.
I no longer bleed for people who wouldn't hand me a damn Band-Aid.
I no longer sit at tables where I have to starve to feel seen.

I am too loud. Too much. Too ambitious.
And too fucking powerful to shrink for comfort.

I don't need closure. I need champagne.
I don't need a second chance. I need a second empire.
I don't chase. I command.

This isn't confidence.
This is a goddamn resurrection.
I buried the version of me that begged—
and I crowned the one who builds thrones from rock bottom.

I'm not waiting for the glow-up.
I AM THE GLOW-UP.

And I am, without question,
WORTHY AS FUCK.

Sign Below to Make It Official.

_____

This isn't just ink—it's your identity now.
Signature of the Worthy AF You:

Date You Claimed Your Throne: _____

Dear Reader,

If you're holding this book right now—you made it. Through the chaos. Through the shame. Through the heartbreak, gaslighting, people-pleasing, emotional landmines, and generational bullshit no one taught you how to navigate. And guess what?

You didn't just survive it. You burned that shit down and built something better. You.

This book wasn't how-to. It was a war cry. A mirror. A permission slip soaked in gasoline. Because I know what it's like to live in survival mode so long that you forget you were born for more than just coping.

You were never broken, babe.
You were just buried under years of bullshit.

Buried under expectations.
Under shame.
Under roles you never chose.
Under the stories they told about who you should be.

And now? You've clawed your way out of that rubble with bloody hands and a voice that won't be silenced ever again. This isn't your soft girl era. This is your sovereign bitch era.

Let the world call you too loud, too much, too intense—good. That means you're finally full of yourself.
And after everything you've been through, you should be.

You don't owe anyone an apology for your glow-up.

You don't need to explain your boundaries, your energy, or your peace.
You've earned every fucking inch of your healing. And it's only just beginning.

So here's what I want you to know:

Don't go back to who you were before.
Don't try to squeeze into spaces you've outgrown.
Don't ever again let someone else's opinion outrank your own damn truth.
This isn't the end of your story.
This is the rebirth.

Now go be louder. Be bolder. Be fucking legendary.

And when you forget who you are—come back to these pages. I'll be right here.
Reminding you what it means to be Worthy As Fuck.

With fire, truth, and zero apologies,
Brandee Kocsis
Founder of the Worthy AF Movement Your mirror. Your hype woman. Your sister in the revolution.

Acknowledgments

To my mom, Debbie—thank you for always supporting my wildest dreams, fiercest rants, and endless shenanigans. When I doubted myself, you were the voice reminding me that I could. When the world told me to quiet down, you reminded me why I shouldn't give a damn what anyone else thinks. Your love gave me roots, and your belief in me gave me wings.

To my daughter, Ryah—you are my why. Watching you become the bold, brilliant, no-apologies version of yourself inspired me to become Worthy AF. I healed so you'd never have to inherit my pain. I rose so you'd never feel guilty for rising higher. You've shattered every ceiling they tried to place above you—and every time I see you break one, I find the courage to smash another of my own. You are powerful, radiant, and made to take up space. Don't ever shrink, baby girl.

To my ride-or-die crew: Kelly, Bobbi, Brandi, Mandy, Shauna, Erin, Stacey, and Tiffany—you've talked me off emotional ledges, called me on my bullshit, and reminded me who the fuck I am. You didn't just hype me up—you held me up. You didn't let me spiral—you snapped me out of it, handed me a coffee, and told me to write the damn book. Each of you shaped this journey, and I'm forever grateful. I love you all more than you know.

To my dad—thank you for telling me, over and over, that I could be anything I wanted to be. Even when I took the long way, the hard way, and the WTF way, you still said, "You've got this, kid." You taught me grit, resilience, and how to get back up swinging. I know you're still with me, cheering from above, watching every bold move. I love you.

To my husband—thank you for growing with me, for growing on your own, and for having patience while I built a brand, a book, and a badass empire with 100 tabs open in my brain. You've supported every wild idea—even when I needed reeling in. You held me accountable without ever dimming my fire. Thank you for always showing up, standing beside me, and believing in this—in me.

And finally—to you, the reader.

You didn't just read this book. You lived it.
You walked through the fire with me.
You cried, cringed, cracked open, and came out more powerful than you ever thought possible.

Thank you for turning the page, doing the work, and choosing to remember who the fuck you are.
You are Worthy As Fuck—always have been, always will be.

This book isn't just mine anymore.
It's yours now.

Let it be the beginning of your next chapter.
Let it be the permission slip you were waiting for.
And when you forget your power, come back here. I'll still be shouting it for you.

With love, fire, and no fucks left to give,
Brandee

About the Author

Brandee Kocsis is a mindset alchemist, trauma-informed mentor, self-worth strategist, and a practicing nurse with over 13 years of experience helping people heal—phsically, emotionally, and energetically. She's the founder of the Worthy AF movement: a revolution for every woman who's ever been told to quiet down, stay small, or settle for scraps.

Brandee's not here for surface-level self-help. Her work is deep, unfiltered, and grounded in real-life experience. After surviving trauma, infertility, toxic relationships, burnout, addiction (yes, even to chocolate), and identity-shattering chaos, she didn't just "find herself"—she rebuilt herself. Louder. Freer. On fire.

She blends mindset rewiring, nervous system healing, and straight-up truth-telling to help women stop performing their worth—and start living it. No fluff. No filters. Just freedom.

She's not your guru. She's your mirror.
And if you're ready to face your shit and rise? She's the one who'll hand you the match.

When she's not writing, coaching, or waking the internet up with a truth bomb, you'll find her sipping iced coffee or margaritas, Rallying the girl gang for spontaneous shenanigans and zero regrets." dancing in her kitchen, and giving her husband endless car concerts, and raising a daughter who's already shattering glass ceilings with her bare hands.

Follow her on Instagram @iam_worthyaf and join the movement that's redefining healing, power, and what it means to be Worthy As Fuck.

www.ingramcontent.com/pod-product-compliance
Lightning Source LLC
Chambersburg PA
CBHW050327010526
44119CB00050B/701